ichi, hitotsu	ni, futatsu	san,
一	二	三
one	two	three

san, mairu			
参			
#participate #three	together	big	#three #join

yon, shi, yotsu			
四			
four			

go, itsutsu			
五			
five	three		five

roku, mutsu, mui		
六		
six		

shichi, nanatsu, nana		
七		
seven		

hachi, yatsu, you		
八		
eight		

juu, tou, ju		
十		
ten	$5 + 5 = 10 \Rightarrow$ + ten	

kyū, ku, kokonotsu				
九	十 -1	十 ⊥	十⊥	九
nine	10-1=9			
zen'				
染	(water)	九	(tree)	(9 colors)
dyeing	water	nine	tree	9 colors
gan, maru, marui				
丸	9	9	(hook)	丸
bend				
gō				
合	(pot)	合		
combine	combine a bowl with a lid			
shuu, jū, hirou				
拾	拾	合		
#ten #pick up	5+5=10(十)	pick up with two hands		

- 3 -

hyaku				
百	ㅏoo		百	百
hundred				

sen, chi			
千	十	'	**1,000**
thousand	ten		

shin, hari			
針			十
needle	iron	needle	

sakana, gyo, uo			
魚			魚
fish			

gyo, ryō			
漁	ミ	シ	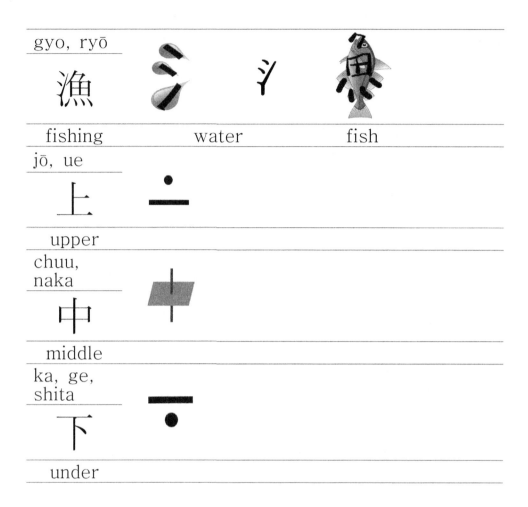
fishing	water	fish	
jō, ue			
上	・―		
upper			
chuu, naka			
中			
middle			
ka, ge, shita			
下	― ●		
under			

shou, ko, chiisai		
小		
small		

jin, nin, hito	
人	
people	

dai, tai, ō	
大	
big	

ten, ama, ame	
天	
sky	

nuke, batsu, nukeru 抜			
pull out	pull out from a big one		
atatakai, dan 暖			
warm	pull out pull your hand out in the sunlight		
kyo 巨			
giant			
san, yama 山			
mountain			

ishi, seki, shaku		
石		
stone		

iwa, gan		
岩		
rock		

shō		小 少
少		

	small	smaller
less	a smaller amount of ⇨ less	

sa, sha, suna		少
砂		

	stone	smaller
sand	#smaller stones #sand	

shi, ko			
子			
child			

ji, aza			
字			
word	home	child	learns at home

gaku, manabu		
学		
learn	learn for glory	

nen, toshi		
年		
year	hand	

jitsu, nichi, hi 日				
day	Sun, day			

shimeru, shitsu 湿			显	
wet	Sun	to shine	obvious	water
	a obvious drop of water			

atatakai, on 温				
temperature	bowl	Sun	water	
	#warm #temperature			

kyū 旧				旧
old	old pictures			

ji, ni		
児	旧	

child	past	child
	past childhood	

katsugu, tan, ninau		
担		

burden

chuu, hiru		
昼		

noon	morning	sundial
	daytime	

sen		
宣		

declare

tsuki 月	moon	meat	body
mei, min', akarui 明	bright	Sun — moon #the sun and the moon #bright	
i 胃	stomach	body — stomach	
kata, ken 肩	shoulder		
ude, wan 腕	arm	#arm #workmanship	

ka, hi

火 火    灬

fire

tou, hi

灯

light

sui, mizu

水

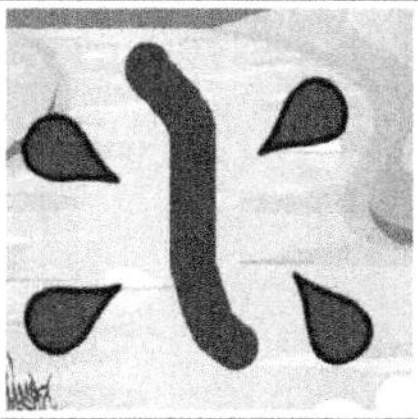

water

eki

益 水 木 宀 今

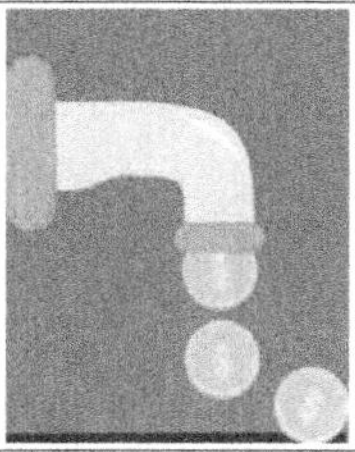

benefit | bowl | overflowing

#overflowing #beyond cost #benefit

moku, boku, ki

木

wood

matsu				
松	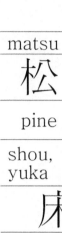	 公	木	
pine		share together	tree	

shou, toko, yuka

松 床

bed

ei, sakae, hae

栄

glory

kyuu, yasumi, yasumu

休

rest

bō

棒

rod

jou, nori, noseru	木	乗	乗	乗

乗

ride   ride a tree

yuu

郵

mail   ride   to the hill, to the ground

satsu, fuda

札

banknotes   banknotes hanging on a tree to dry

ki, tsukue

机

machine

kabu

株

stock   #base of tree #stock company

hada 肌		几	
skin	body	cover	
sho 処		夂	
place		go	bench
jō 条			
article	go	wooden pencil	
kin, kon, kane 金			
money	iron, gold, money		
ushinau, shitsu 失		矢	失
miss	arrow	slip out	
tetsu 鉄	失		金
iron	slip out	iron	

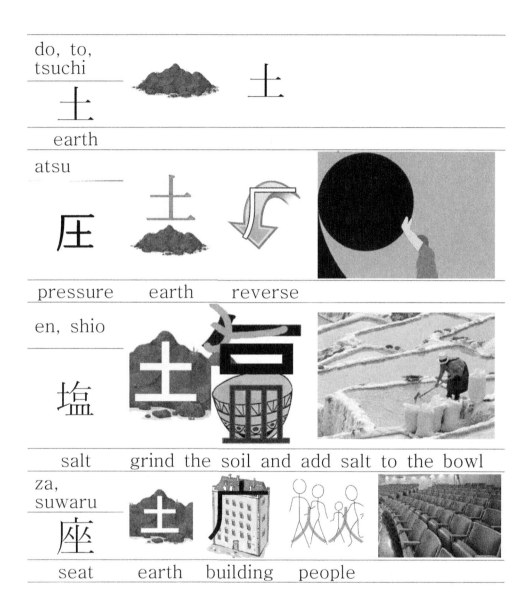

do, to, tsuchi 土		
earth		
atsu 圧		
pressure	earth	reverse
en, shio 塩		
salt	grind the soil and add salt to the bowl	
za, suwaru 座		
seat	earth	building	people

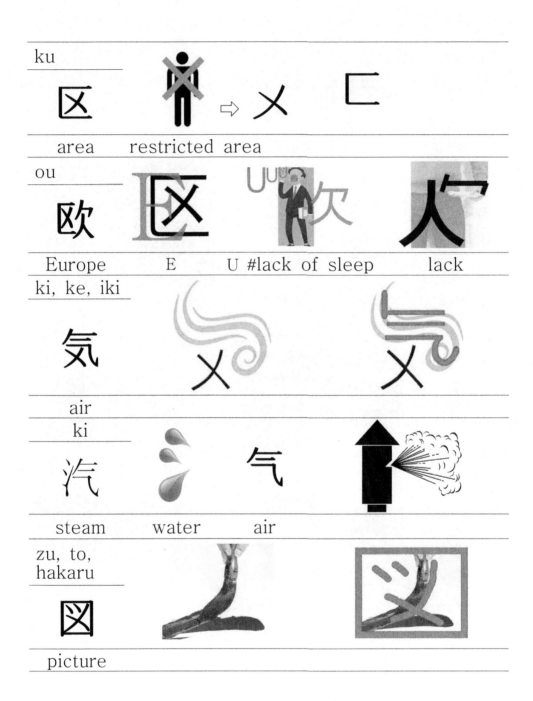

ku

区

area   restricted area

ou

欧

Europe   E   U #lack of sleep   lack

ki, ke, iki

気

air

ki

汽

steam   water   air

zu, to,
hakaru

図

picture

nō			
脳		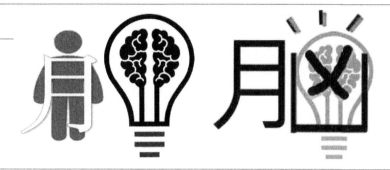	
brain			

忄		心	
heart			

nayamasu, nō, nayamu				
悩				
distress	psychological pressure			

kyou, mune, muna		
胸	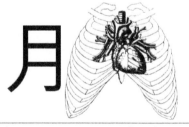	
chest	heart wrapped chest	

ryoku, riki, chikara	
力	
power	

rō 労	labor	labor powerfully for glory

ka, kuwaeru, kuwawaru 加	add	power	speak

#speak powerfully #add praise

kyō 協	cooperation

dan, otoko 男	man	man working in the field

殳			又	几
		hand		stand

a tool in one's hand
to make something by hands

dan 段	𣪊	𣪊	殳
segment	stairs	make	tool
	divide by stairs		

korosu, satsu, sai 殺		乄木	殳
kill	kill with tools		

setsu, moukeru 設		言	殳
setting	speak		make
	make as directed		

tou, nage 投			扌	殳
throw		hand		tool
	throw with a tool			

役			イ	殳
eki, yaku				
role		walk		tool
walk with tools and play a role				

共				共
tomo				
together	#put one's hands together #together			

展			衣	
ten'				
exhibition	cart	hand	clothe	

殿	殳	共		
ten, den, tono				
palace	tool	together	cart	

入				
nyuu, iri, hairu				
enter				

込		之	入	
komi, komeru				
included		walk	enter	

uchi, nai, dai 内	入	冂
inside	enter	inside

ryō 両	両 ①	両 ① ②	両
both			

man, michiru, mitasu 満	両		
full	both	grass	water

kai 貝				貝
money	shellfish	shiny shellfish	money, wealth	

ou, fu, makeru 負			ク	貝
negative		bend		money

#debt #to owe money #negative

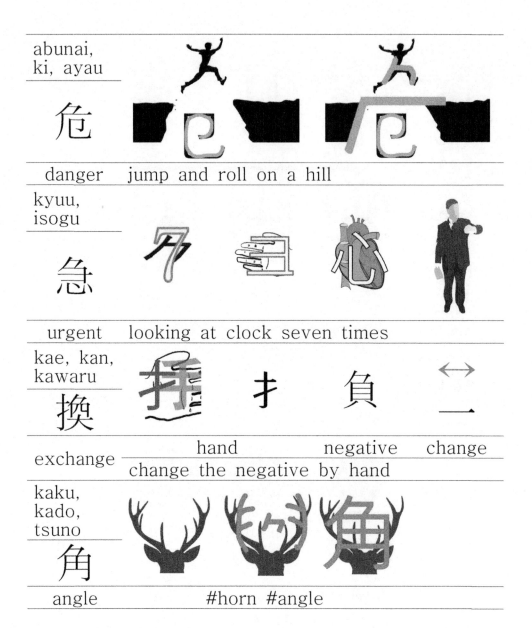

abunai, ki, ayau 危		
danger	jump and roll on a hill	

kyuu, isogu 急			
urgent	looking at clock seven times		

kae, kan, kawaru 換			
	hand	negative	change
exchange	change the negative by hand		

kaku, kado, tsuno 角		
angle	#horn #angle	

ushi				
牛				
cattle				

kai, tokeru, toku				
解	角	牛		
solve	horn	cattle	knife	
	solve a cattles horn with a knife			

chū, mushi			
虫			
worm			

sawaru, shoku, fure			
触		角	虫
touch	#horn #antennae	worm	
	#worm #antennae #touch		

fuu, fu, kaze			
風			
wind			

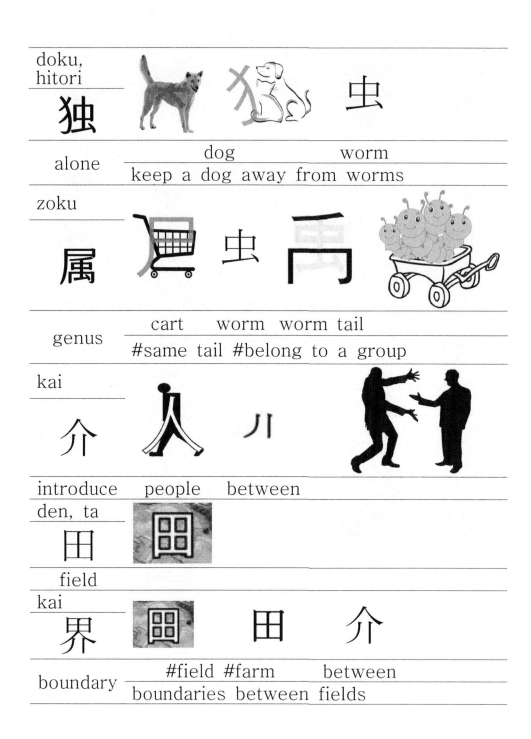

doku, hitori 独		虫
alone	dog	worm
	keep a dog away from worms	

zoku 属		虫	
genus	cart	worm worm tail	
	#same tail #belong to a group		

kai 介	人	川
introduce	people	between

den, ta 田	
field	

kai 界	田	介
boundary	#field #farm	between
	boundaries between fields	

sei, se, yo 世		一　　せ　　せ　　世

generation

	10 years	20 years	30 years

#30 years #one generation #world

ha, yō 葉			世

leaf

tree	grass	generation

a leaf that changes generations

tan 単		

single　a slingshot that hunts alone

hata, hatake 畑			

field	fire	field	

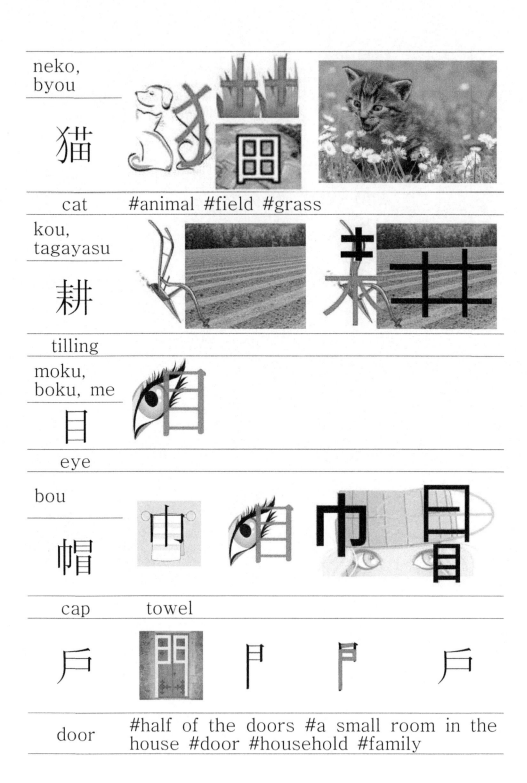

neko, byou		
猫		
cat	#animal #field #grass	
kou, tagayasu		
耕		
tilling		
moku, boku, me		
目		
eye		
bou		
帽		
cap	towel	
戸		
door	#half of the doors #a small room in the house #door #household #family	

- 28 -

ko, yatoi		隹		

雇

hire — hang it on the door like a bird

sui

推

guess — bird   hand
as guess, pigeon in hand

shin,
susumu,
susumeru

進

 辶 隹

advance — walk   bird
bird can't fly backwards. only forward!

gyaku,
sakarau,
saka

逆

reverse

jun

準

level — level that won't fall into the water

shuu,
atsumeru

集

collect

seki

隻

ship　　words to count the number of ships

kaku,
tashika,
tashikameru

確

certainly　certainly safe

ken

権

authority　pen made of bird feathers

zatsu, zou	
雑	
miscellaneous	nine kinds of birds are mixed on the tree ⇨ miscellaneous

hon	
本	
this	#roots #basis #origin #this

tai, karada, katachi	
体	
body	person basis
	the basis of a person

chou, tori	
鳥	
bird	

kou, ku,
kuchi

口

mouth

naku,
mei,
naru

鳴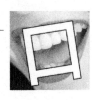

#ringing #croak

shima,
tou

島 山 鳥

island   mountain   bird

go, tagai

互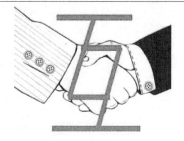

mutual

gou

号

口　万

number ——— say　curve
call according to the number

mo

以

therefore　I dropped it therefore it broke

ji, nni

似　　以

similar ——— person　therefore
he is my son, therefore he resembles me.

gyoku,
tama

玉

　　王　玉

bead

ou		
王		
king	#jade #king	

takara, hou		
宝		
treasure		

koku, kuni			
国	口	王	
country	fence	#jade #king	
	#a fence with a king #nation		

han'		
班		
group	#divide #class #group	

ken, inu		
犬		犭
dog		

utsuwa, kki 器		器
device	#the dog is monitoring all directions #monitoring device	

ana 穴	宀	ㅆ	八
hole	house	hand	
	#a house dug by hand #cave #hole		

tsuku, to 突	穴	犬
sudden	hole	dog
	dog suddenly comes out of the hole	

zen, nen 然		
but	the dog wants to eat meat. but the fire is hot	

nen, moeru, moyasu 燃	然	火
ignite	but	fire
	but set on fire	

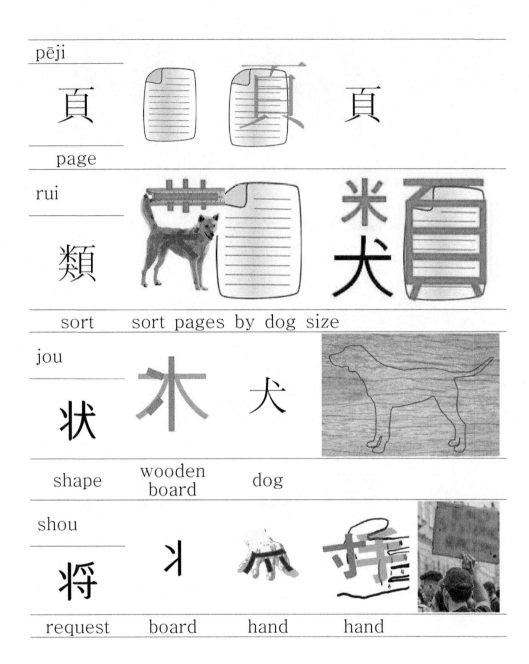

pēji

頁

page

rui

類

sort sort pages by dog size

jou

状

shape wooden board dog

shou

将

request board hand hand

shin, ne, nekasu		
寝		

sleeping

kata, hen		
片	木	朼

piece

kan		
缶		

canister

niku		
肉		

meat

i		
胃		

stomach   body   stomach

tora 虎 tiger	
hada 膚 skin	虍　　胃 tiger　　stomach skin except for the tiger's stomach
geki 劇 drama	#tiger #pig #sword
ka, ya, ie 家 home	
ke, mou 毛 hair	#wool #hair

don, nibui, niburu			
鈍			
dull	iron	hang	
	#only hang #become dull		

jun			
純			
pure	string	hang	
	#clean #pure		

taku			
宅			
home	house	hang	

kou, takai		
高		
high		

kyou, hashi		
橋		
bridge	high frame	

shou, zou	
象	
shape	#long nose #wide ears #thick legs like pigs #elephant #shape

zou		
像	象	
statue	person shape	

ban		
晩		
night	sun avoid #the sun sets(avoid) #night	

ben, tsutomu 勉	
study	avoid　　　power #avoid other work #study hard

gyuu, ushi 牛	
bull	

ken 件	
clothes　　person　　cattle	

butsu, motsu, mono 物	
object	#beef products #goods #object

ji 寺	
office	land　　　　#hand #manage #manage the land #government office

toku 特	牛	寺
	cattles	government office
particular	#cattles used for government events #special #particular	

hitsuji 羊	
sheep	#excellent #sacrificed

you 洋		シ	羊
	water		excellent
foreign	#excellent water #ocean #foreign		

utsukushi i, bi 美	羊	主		大
	excellent			big
nice	#big and excellent #nice			

sama, you 様		羊 水	
looks	excellent tree and water		

ware

我

I

gi

議

discussion

tatsu, tachi

達

reach   reach earth with the sheep

okureru, chi, oso

遅

late   why holding sheep?

sa, sasu

差

different different make

- 43 -

chaku, jyaku, gi 着	sheep eye	
wear	sheep's skin, wolf eyes	
jo, on'na 女		
female		
an, yasu 安	home	#female #mother
safe	I'm safe at home with my mother	
bo, haha, kaa 母		
mother		
goto 毎	一 母 毋	
every	hand mother	
	mom's hand every time	

kai, umi 海			
sea	water	every	
	sea where every water gathers		

baku, mugi 麦			
wheat	wheat	go	
	#harvest wheat #wheat		

kou, konomu, suku 好	女	子	子
it is good	mother	child	
	#the mother is holding the child #it is good		

yatsu 奴	女		又
slave	mother	hand	
	slave to replace your mother's hand		

tsutomu, do			
努	奴	力	力
to exert	slave	power	
	to work as hard as a slave		

ikaru, do, okoru		
怒	奴	心
angry	slave	heart

fu, chichi, tou		
父		
father		

otto, fu, fuu		
夫		
husband		

ki			
規	夫		
rule	husband	see	

san			
賛		夫夫	
praise	gift	adult	
	praise with gifts		

kae, tai, kawaru			
替	夫夫		
replace	adult	say	

tē, hikui, hikumeru			
低			
low	root	person	
	#plant the roots of plants #low		

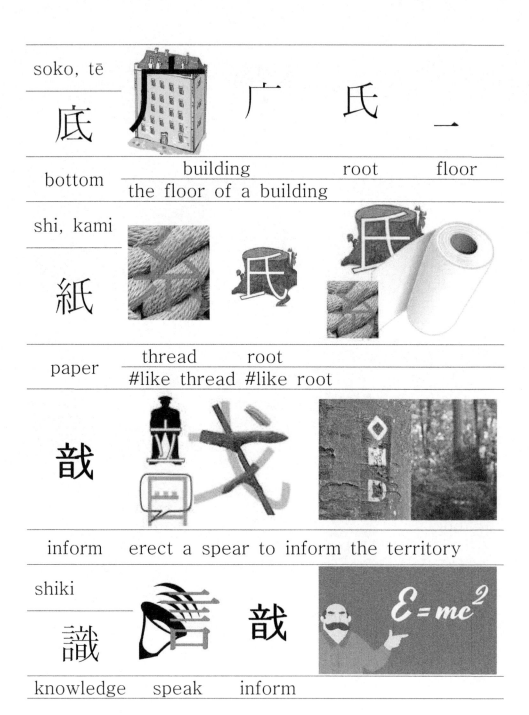

soko, tē

底

bottom · building · root · floor

the floor of a building

---

shi, kami

紙

paper · thread · root

#like thread #like root

戠

inform · erect a spear to inform the territory

---

shiki

識

knowledge · speak · inform

nin, mitomeru 認		
approval		
shoku 職	戠	
	job ear inform	
kon 婚	女	
marriage	until my black hair becomes green onion roots	
ppanashi, hou, hanatsu 放	芳 攵	
release	direction hit with a stick	
geki 激	放	
intense water release white		

旁	方		

flag

direction   #hand #hang

flags hung to show directions

ryo, tabi

旅

journey

zoku

族

flag   arrow

clan

clan territory marked with flags and arrows

asobu, yuu

遊

play   walk   child   flag

sono

其

it

sticky note (post-it)   table

#post-it on the table #it

ki		
基	土	其
basic	earth	it
	basic on the ground	

ki, go		
期	其	月
period	it	#moon #month
	month that	

ri		
里		
village		

dou, warabe		
童	里	
child	village stand	
	child runs in the village	

hakaru, ryō		
量	里	
amount morning village		

- 51 -

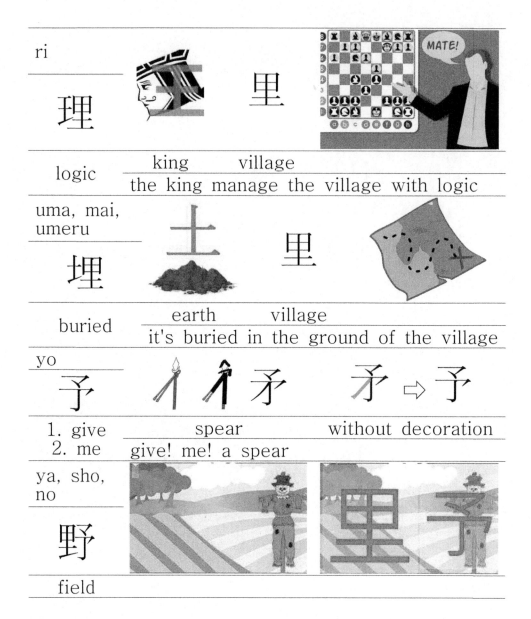

ri 理	logic	king	village
		the king manage the village with logic	

uma, mai, umeru 埋	buried	earth	village
		it's buried in the ground of the village	

yo 予	1. give 2. me	spear	without decoration
		give! me! a spear	

| ya, sho, no 野 | field | | |

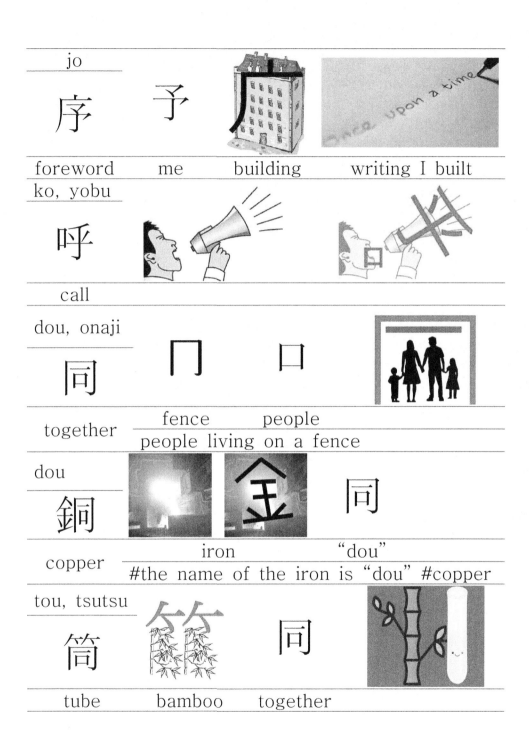

jo			
序	予	庁	writing
foreword	me	building	writing I built

ko, yobu		
呼		
call		

dou, onaji			
同	冂	口	
together	fence	people	
	people living on a fence		

dou			
銅		同	
copper	iron	"dou"	
	#the name of the iron is "dou" #copper		

tou, tsutsu		
筒	同	
tube	bamboo	together

u, ama, ame			
雨			
rain			

setsu, yuki			
雪			
snow			

den			
電	雨	电	
electricity	rain	lightning	

wan, kumo			
雲	雨	云	
cloud	rain	cloud	

kumori, don			
曇		雲	
cloudy	sun	cloud	

kai, e, au			
会		云	
meet	combine	cloud	

e, kai 絵	thread	会	
picture		meet	
gē 芸	grass	cloud	performing arts
art			
ten 転	car #turn #driving #rotation		
roll			
den, tsutau, tsutaeru 伝	person	cloud	
legend			
sen, kawa 川			
river			
shuu, su 州			
state			

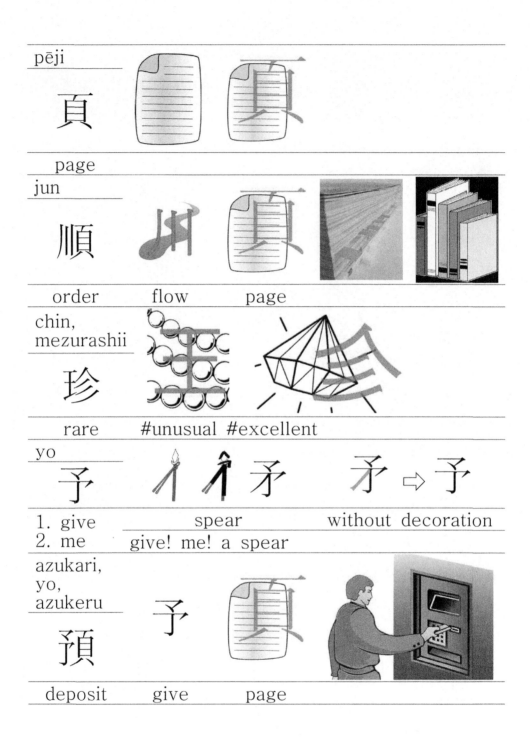

pēji		
頁		
page		

jun		
順		
order	flow	page

chin, mezurashii		
珍		
rare	#unusual	#excellent

yo		
予		
1. give 2. me	spear	without decoration
	give! me! a spear	

azukari, yo, azukeru		
預		
deposit	give	page

- 56 -

tsutomeru, mu			
務			
duties	#spear #hit #power #active military service		

amasu, yo, amari			
余			
surplus	tree	combine	

to, nuri				
塗				
paint	water	surplus	earth	#mud #paint

to		
途		
on the way	walk	surplus

walking from one place to another place

ji, jo, nozoku			
除	阝	余	
remove	hill	surplus	

kieru, shou, kesu		
消		
remove	belly fat removal	

sha, suteru				
捨	扌	古	合	
discard	hand	ancient	combine	discard
	discard old stuff			

cha, sa			
茶		茶	
tea	tea on a wooden table		

kaku, ketsu, kakeru			
欠			
lack			

shi, ji, tsugi			
次			
second	lack		second

shi				貝	次
資					
fund		money			second
	first, second, raise money				

tou, nusumu	資	資	盗	盗
盗				
theft	fund		theft	

sui, fuki			
吹			
boast	lack	mouth	

kan, nareru, narasu 慣				
	money	goods	heart	
custom	exchange of money and goods is customary			

jitsu, mi, minoru 実			
	fruit	house	grip

kan, wazurau 患			
affliction	pierce	heart	

fun, bun, wakaru 分		
divide		

ko, fun, kona 粉	✳	米	分
powder	small	divide	
	to divide into very small pieces		

hin, bin, mazushii 貧	分	
poor	money	divide
	poor because of the divide in money	

shin, kokoro 心	
heart	

shi, omoe 思	田	田心	思
think	thoughts in my heart		

aku, warui 悪	press down	heart
evil	evil that presses the heart	

shuu, fune, funa 舟			舟
boat			

殳			又　几
tool		hand	stand

hatsu 般	舟	殳	
sort	boat	tool	

sen', fune, funa 船	舟		
ship	boat		ship

kou		
航	舟	
sailing	boat	

seki, shaku, aka		
赤	土 火	
red		

mata		
亦	again? 亦	
once more	arms folded	

ato, seki		
跡	足 亦	
traces	leg once more	

kaeru, hen, kawaru		
変	亦	
odd	one more walk	
	are they walking together?	

koi, ren, koishii			
恋	亦		
love	once more	heart	

wan			
湾	亦		
bay	once more	longbow	

waves on the bow hill once more

hi		
陽		
sunshine		

jou, chou, ba		
場		
field		

tou, yu	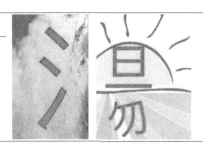
湯	
hot water	

futsu, waku, nie	 
沸	
boiling	

tsuieru, hi, tsuiyasu	 
費	
expense money	

i, eki, yasu	 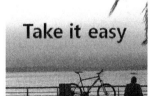
易	
easy	

uru, toku, eru 得 obtain		
	#morning旦 #hand寸 #walk彳 #obtain.	

seki, yuu 夕 evening		

gai, hoka, soto 外 outside	夕 evening	 lock the door
	#lock the door in the evening and go out #outside	

ya, yo, yoru 夜 night	夕 evening	 clothes	衣 ⇨ 仓 can't see the clothes
	a night when you can't see all of your clothes		

eki 液		シ	夜
liquid		water	night
	alcohol at night ⇨ liquid		

mu, yume 夢			++ / 夕
dreams			

mei, myou, na 名	夕		口
name	evening	call	
	call out a name to identify someone on a dark evening		

onoono, kaku 各	夂		
each	go	entrance	
	each entrance		

kaku, kou			
格		各	
standard	wood	each	

karamaru, raku, karamu			
絡		各	
connection	thread	each	

ochi, raku, otosu			
落	各		
drop	each	grass	water
	the leaves drop on the water		

ryaku			
略	各		
slightly	each	field	

ji, ro			
路	各	足	
road	each	leg	

kaku, kyaku		
客	各	宀
customer	each	home
	a customer who came home	

gaku, hitai		
額	客	
amount	customer	page
	#customer #money amount	

atama, tou, zu		
頭		
head	page	bowl

tan, mijikai 短	arrow		bowl	豆
short	the arrow you put into the bowl is short			

hou, yutaka 豊	豆	曲	
rich	bowl	full	

doku 毒	母		grass
poison	mother	grass	the poison grass that my mother shouldn't eat

gai 害	house	poison	mouth 口
harmful	house	poison	mouth
	it's harmful to keep poison grass at home		

katsu, wari, saku 割	害	knife	
discount	harmful	knife	
	cut out defective products and sell at a discount		

ao				
青				
blue	grass grows		sprout	
	#the sprouts have grown green #blue			

sei			
清	青		
clear	blue	water	#blue water #clear water

sei			
精	青	米	
spirit	clear	small	small and shiny

jō			
情	心	青	
affection	heart	clear	transparent mind

me			
芽		牙	
sprout	tooth	grass	
	tooth-shaped sprouts		

sai, matsuri, matsuru			
祭			
festival	#eat #show #play		

kiwa, sai			
際	阝	祭	
edge	hill	festival	

sasshi			
察	宀	祭	
guess	house	festival	
	what kind of show?		

gyou, gou, waza			
業			
work	wooden musical instrument		
	work like a musical instrument		

ki, yorokobu			
喜			
pleasure	drum and sing		

oto, on, ne		
音		
sound	stand	say

an, kurai		
暗		音
dark	sun	sound
	no light. only sound	

i		
意	音	

meaning	sound	heart
	sound expressed from the heart	

oku		
億		意

billion	person	meaning
	how many thoughts do people have? billion	

kiwamu		
竟	音	音

in the end	sound	the end of the sound

kyou, kei, sakai		
境	土	竟

border	earth	end

shou 章	立	日	十	
chapter	stand	word	#ten #many	chapter with many words

sara 皿			
dish		bowl	

ketsu, chi 血	皿	◣ 皿	
blood	bowl	put in	
	blood in a bowl (for ancestral rites)		

komaru, kon 困	口	木	
sleepy	fence	wood	
	sleeping on a wooden fence		

in, yoru 因	口	大	
because	fence	big	
	why did the big one get into the fence? because ~		

on		
恩	因	
favor	because	heart
	the desire to help for some reason	

i, kakomu, kakoi	
囲	
enclosure	

uyamau, kei	
敬	
respect	

kei	
警	
police	#attention #gun #sound

tsutsumu, hou		
包	巳	巳 勹
package	bend over	pack
	bending and packing	

idaku, hou, daku 抱		包	
hug	hand	package	

iru, you 要			
want	cover		female
	the woman wants to cover up		

koshi, you 腰		要	
waist	body	want	

en, kemuri, kemuru 煙		火	里
smoke			

ken			
券			
ticket	grip	knife	grip and cut

katsu, shou, masaru			
勝			
win	body	power	grip

kan, maku, maki			
巻			
roll	stand	grip	

癶			
walk			

to, tou, noboru			
登		癶	
climbing	bowl	walk	

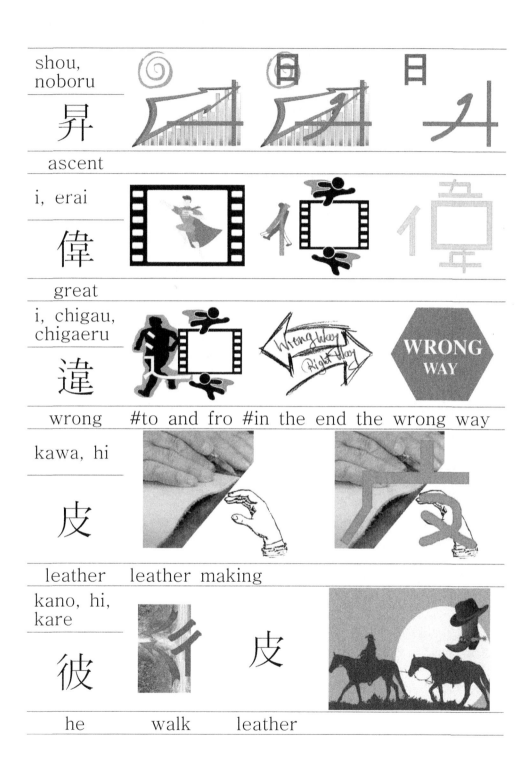

shou, noboru	
昇	
ascent	
i, erai	
偉	
great	
i, chigau, chigaeru	
違	
wrong	#to and fro #in the end the wrong way
kawa, hi	
皮	
leather	leather making
kano, hi, kare	
彼	
he	walk leather

- 79 -

疒
sick

疲
tsukareru,
hi

疒 + 皮
exhaustion sick leather blisters on lips

被
koumuru,
hi,
kaburu

衤 + 皮
by clothes leather step by step

波
nami, ha

氵 + 皮
wave water leather

shí 石		
stone	rock (石 right)	

ha, yaburu, yabureru 破	石　　皮	
break	stone　　leather	
	stone damaged leather	

ha 派		
faction	#water　divides　#a　faction　forms	
	#T-group, E-group, C-group	

艮		
wear	hand	wear

fuku 服		艮
serve	body	wear

kou, saiwai, shiawase 幸		
	fortunately	fortunately landed

hou, mukuiru 報		
① report ② revenge	#wear fortunately news on paper #report	#fortunately catch the criminal #wear prisoner's uniform #pay for one's crime

kaku, kawa 革	十		苗
leather	many		trim
	leather with many trimming		

化	人			

transform #change into #convert

ka, kutsu			
靴	革	化	
shoes	leather	transform	

obi, tai, obiru				
帯	巾		常	市
belt				

tou, higashi			
東		木日	木 日
east			

kooru, tou, kogoeru			
凍		東	
frozen	ice	east	

soku, taba 束	木	口	
bundle	wood	bundle	

sumiyaka, soku, hayai 速	束	(walk)	
speed	bundle	walk	

tanomu, rai, tanomoshii 頼	束	頁	
rely	bundle	page	rely on money

neru, ren 練	(thread)	束	(insert)	
training	thread	bundle	insert	weaving training

sasaru, shi, sasu 刺	朿	刂	
prick	thorn	knife	

saku 策	筥	朿	
plan	bamboo	prick	

sei, sai, nishi 西		
west	west where the sun sets	

sake, shu 酒		酉
wine	water	wine vessel

nan, minami 南	羊	巿	
south	sheep	fence	
	southern pasture		

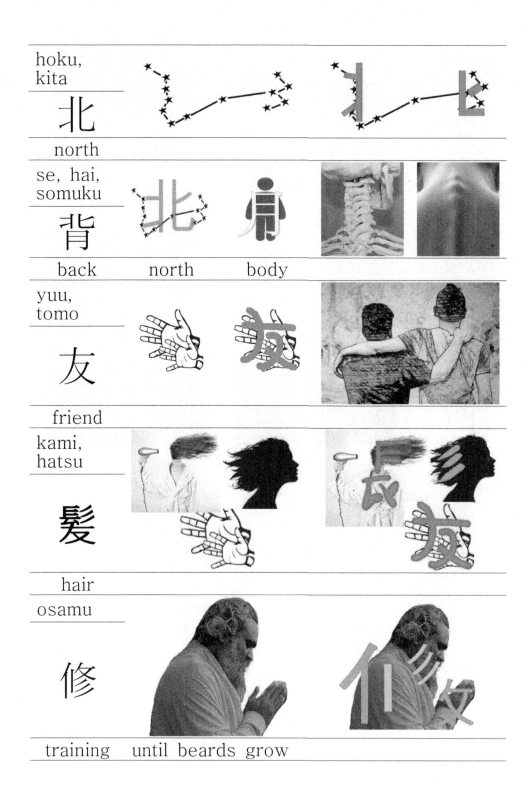

hoku, kita			
北			
north			
se, hai, somuku			
背			
back	north	body	
yuu, tomo			
友			
friend			
kami, hatsu			
髪			
hair			
osamu			
修			
training	until beards grow		

sa, hidari — 左		
left	left hand scissors	

yuu, migi, u — 右		
right side	right hand is a rock	

jaku, wakai — 若		
if	right hand plus hand code	
	if you press it wrong	

shou, sukunai, sukoshi — 少		small smaller
less	a smaller amount of ⇨ less	

byou			
秒		少	
seconds	rice	smaller	small as rice
kaerimiru, sei, shou			
省	少		
ministry	smaller	see	look after people
ito, shi			
糸			
thread			
ku, kou, beni			
紅			
deep red	thread	#work #dye	
moto			
素			
element	grass	thread	

komakai, sai, hosoi			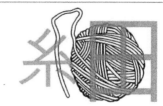
細			

thin

公			ム		八

public	together	divide

#share together #public

sou		公		
総				

total	thread	public	heart

totaling the public mind

売			土 儿 

sell

zoku, tsuzuku, tsuzukeru		売	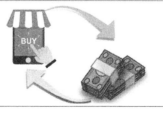
続			

continued	thread	sell

sell and buy, sell and buy, sell and buy

doku, yomi 読	善	続	Read!
reading	speak	continued	

midori, roku 緑	thread	hand	water	
green	#hand #dye thread #color of water			

roku 録	iron	hand	water
record			

yō 幼	thread	#thinner than thread #small	power
young	small power ⇨ young		

go, kou, ato 後	walk	small	walk
later	come later		

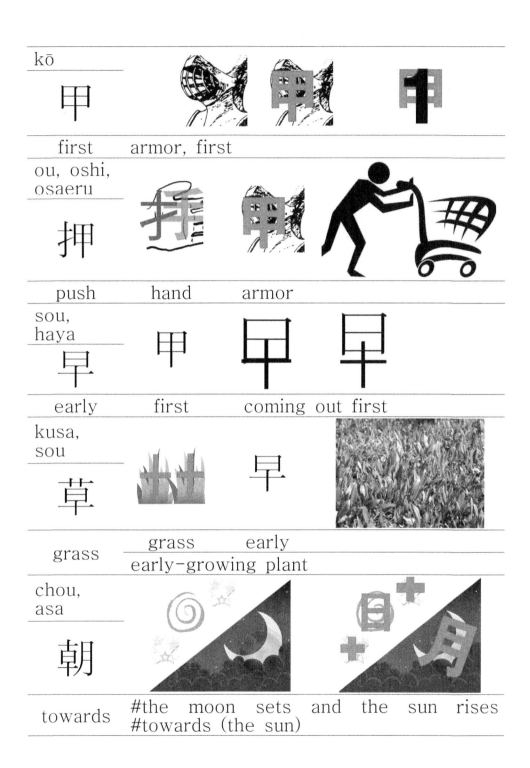

kō		
甲		
first	armor, first	

ou, oshi, osaeru		
押		
push	hand	armor

sou, haya		
早		
early	first	coming out first

kusa, sou		
草		
grass	grass	early
	early-growing plant	

chou, asa		
朝		
towards	#the moon sets and the sun rises #towards (the sun)	

inui, kan, kara		
乾		
dry	water, please~	

baku		
莫		
no more	no more sunshine	

tsunoru, bo		
募	莫	力
recruitment	no more	power
	#has no power #need recruitment	

kurasu, bo, kure		
暮	莫	
end of life	no more	sun

haka, bo		
墓	莫	土
grave	no more	earth

nai, mu, bu	 
無	
nothing	nothing left after incineration

bu, mau, mai	 
舞	
dance	nothing foot invisible foot

chi, nyuu, chichi	
乳	
milk	

ukabu, fu, uku	 
浮	
floating	

zetsu 舌	十	1,000	千	
tongue	ten	thousand		sound
	a tongue that makes a thousand sounds			

midasu, ran, midareru 乱	舌		
disturbance	tongue	thing	

rai, rei 礼			
courtesy	show	thing	

ana 穴		宀	丷	八
hole	#house dug by hand #cave #hole			

kuu, kara, sora 空	穴		工
air	hole		work
	#make a hole #be empty #air		

kyuu, ku, kiwamu			
究	穴		
research	hole	bend over	
	bend over to see the hole		

sou, mado				
窓	穴			
window	hole	together	heart	
	neighboring hearts together			

byou, yamai, yamu				
病			疒	
sick				

ryō				
寮				
torch				

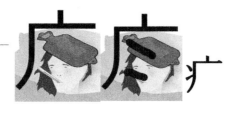

ryō			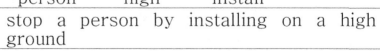
療	疒	尞	
medical treatment	sick	torch	

ryou		
了		
finish		

cho				
貯				
saving	money	house	hammer	

kō		
高		
high		

toma			
停	person	high	install
stop	stop a person by installing on a high ground		

- 96 -

itadaki, chou, itadaku 頂			
top	hammer	page	
	hammering at the top		

utsu, da 打			
beat	hand	hammer	

chou, machi 町			
town	city		build

chou 庁			
office	building	build	

uketama waru, shou 承		手	モ	毛
support	to support with hands and hands			

jou, musu, mureru 蒸	  
steamed	
kyoku, goku, kiwameru 極	 
extreme	
ikusa, sen, tatakau 戦	 
war	
asa, sen 浅	 
shallow	

歹		歺	歹
bad	#broken bones #dead #bad		

zan, nokoru, nokosu 残		歹戋
remainder		

jou, sē, naru 成	戈	戊		丁
to make	spear		hammer	
	to make with a spear and hammer			

jou, shiro 城	成	土	
city	to make	earth	

aru		
或		
maybe	maybe...	

iki		
域	土　或	
area	land　maybe	
	maybe alien territory?	

kai		
械	spear hand	
weapon	a hand-made wooden device to attack	

i		
威		
power		

iku, ki		
幾		
how many		

ki, hata		
機	木	幾

#machine #opportunity	wood	how many
#take out by machine #how many chance?		

shin'				
臣		目	甲	臣
servant	servant who only looks down			

kura, zou		
蔵		
warehouse		

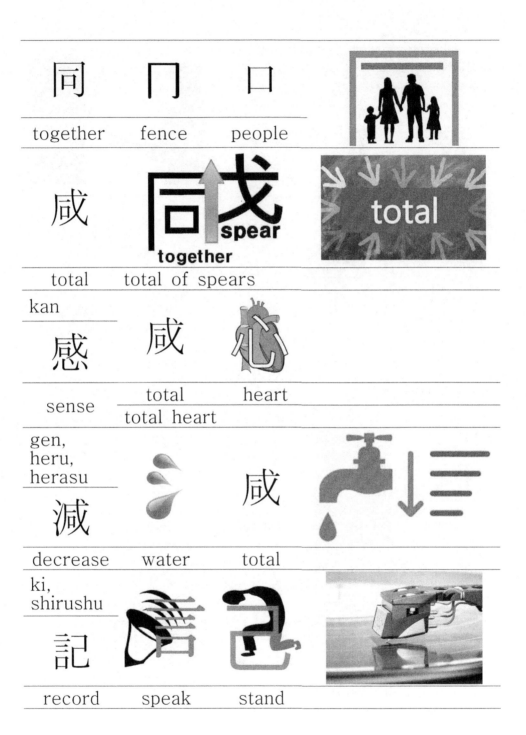

同	冂	口
together	fence	people

咸		
total	total of spears	

kan		
感	咸	
sense	total	heart
	total heart	

gen, heru, herasu		
減		咸
decrease	water	total

ki, shirushu		
記		
record	speak	stand

ki, okiru, okosu			
起			
start	stand up	run	

kubaru, hai			
配			
pair	wine vessel	stand up	
	drink a toast		

san'			
酸	酉	夋	允
acid	wine	go and go again	
	old sour wine		

karashi, shin			
辛		羊	辛
spicy			

舌	十	1,000	千	
tongue	ten	thousand		sound
	a tongue that makes a thousand sounds			

ji, yameru	舌 辛
辞	
speech	fiery speech

nin, makaseru, makasu	
任	

selected	ー	十	イ	'
	line	many	person	select

tei, hodo				
程				
about	rice	mouth	bead	about this much?

shi, tomaru, tome			
止			止
stop			

en, nobe, nobasu 延				
extension	stop	stop and extension		

tei, niwa 庭	延			
garden	extension	building		

ushinau, shitsu 失	矢	失		
miss	arrow	slip out		

chi, shiru 知	矢		口	
know	arrow	word		

to know a word as fast as an arrow

i 医	矢	匚		
medical	arrow	cover		

cover the arrow wound and heal

utagau, gi, utagai 疑		
suspicion	they're all pointy. which one?	

oiru, rou, fukeru 老		老	少
old	#curved back土	#walking stick/	#slow steps匕

kou, kangaeru, kangae 考	少	丂
test	old	question
	old man's question	

sha, mono 者	少	白	
person	old	white	
	old man, white beard		

sho, cho, o 緒		者
cord	string	person
	to beginning with	

sho			
諸	言	者	
various	speak	person	

shi, to, miyako			
都	者	阝	
capital city	person	hill	

atsui, sho			
暑	日	者	
hot	sun	person	

sho			
署	目	者	
office	eye	person	

arawasu,
cho,
ichijirushii

著

show

en

演

perform   #music flowing like water #perform

ou, kou, ki

黄

yellow   perform   the roof of the performance venue is yellow

ou, yoko

横 黄

side   wood   yellow   side menu

chiku	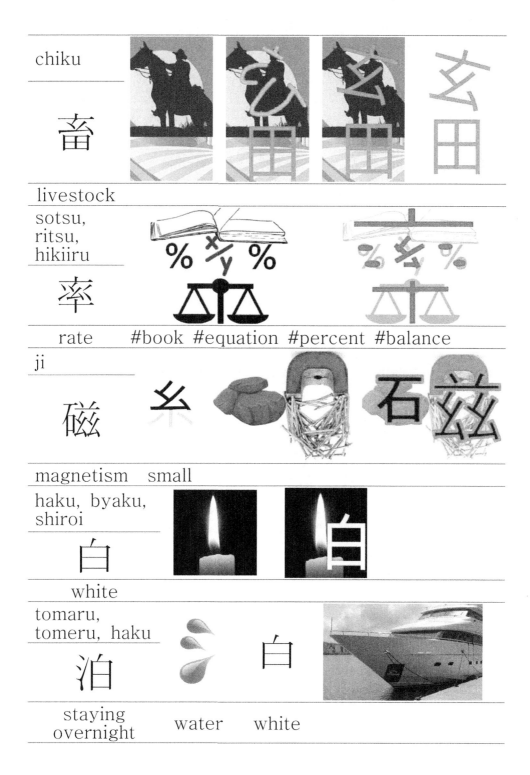			
畜				
livestock				
sotsu, ritsu, hikiiru				
率				
rate	#book	#equation	#percent	#balance
ji				
磁				
magnetism small				
haku, byaku, shiroi				
白				
white				
tomaru, tomeru, haku				
泊		water	white	
staying overnight				

hyaku 百				
hundred				

shuku, yado, yadoru 宿				
lodge for the night	#house #motel	hundred		person
	a person lodge for the night at a motel for a hundred dollars			

zen, mattaku 全		
complete	cover it well so that it's complete without any cracks	

shu, su, nushi 主		
main	main board	

juu, chuu, sumu			
住		主	
dwell	people	main	

chuu, hashira			
柱		主	
pillar	tree	main	

chuu, sosogu, sasu			
注		主	
concentrate	water	main	

kimi, kun				
君			尹	口
		sword in hand		speak
monarch	a monarch who commands with a sword in his hand			

gun, mureru, mure 群	君		
group	monarch	sheep	

kou, sourou 候		矣	
weather	person	arrow	

chuu, naka 仲		中	
relationship	people	middle	

ou 央	中	中	大
central	middle		large

in the middle of a large

ei, utsuru, utsusu 映		◎ 日	央
reflect		Sun	central
	sunlight reflects in the middle		

ei 英		央
English		

in, shirushi 印		
print	imprint rubber stamp	

tamago, ran 卵		卵
egg	frog eggs ⇨ common eggs	

gei,
mukae

迎

welcome

uma, ba,
ma

馬

horse

eki

駅

station | horse | to measure the distance

a station at regular intervals

chuu

駐 馬

resident | horse | main

亼 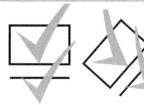  亼

check

gen', tamesu

験　馬　亼

test　horse　check

kewashii, ken

険 亼

rugged　hill　check

ken

検 亼

inspection　board　check

tatsu	辰			
when	when the clouds stay on the hill			

shin, furuu, furueru 震		辰		
quake	rain	when		

nou 農			辰	
agriculture	grain		when	

koi, nou 濃		農		
dark	water	agriculture	#dark #deep	

sue, matsu, batsu 末		末
end	pass the **end** of the tree	

mi 未		未
not yet	the tip of the tree has **not yet** grown	

mai, imouto 妹	女	未	
sister	female	not yet (child)	

shi, ane 姉	女	市	
	female	city	
sister	sisters who lived in the same city as children		

mi, aji 味		未	
	mouth	not yet	
taste	not chew yet		

- 117 -

uma		
午		
noon		
on, gyo, go		
御		
my dear friend	leave school at noon	
kyo, moto		
許	午	
permit	speak noon	
	only during lunch time	
shi, ji, shimese		
示		
show		

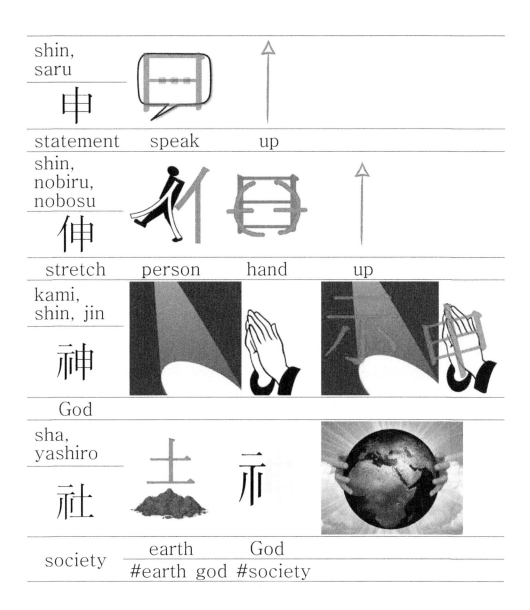

shin, saru 申	statement	speak	up
shin, nobiru, nobosu 伸	stretch	person	hand	up
kami, shin, jin 神	God		
sha, yashiro 社	society	earth	God

#earth god #society

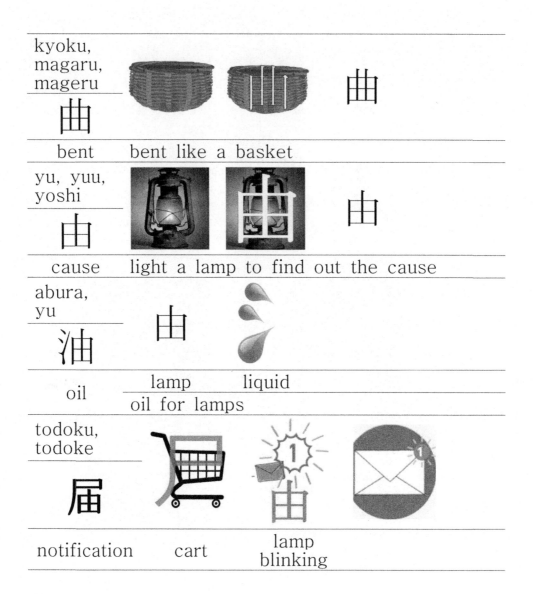

kyoku, magaru, mageru 曲			曲
bent	bent like a basket		

yu, yuu, yoshi 由			由
cause	light a lamp to find out the cause		

abura, yu 油	由		
oil	lamp	liquid	
	oil for lamps		

todoku, todoke 届		由	
notification	cart	lamp blinking	

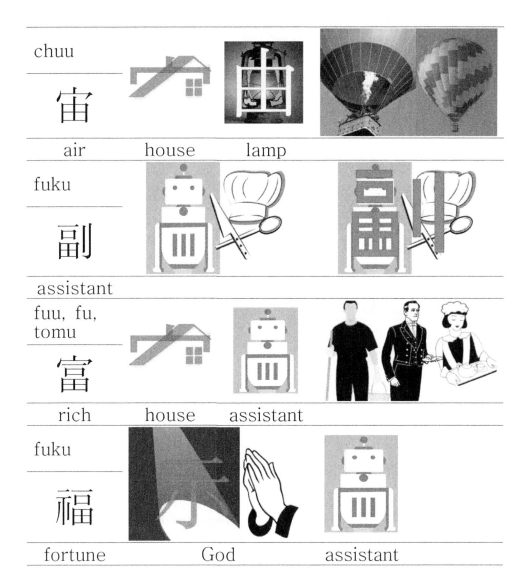

chuu 宙			
air	house	lamp	

fuku 副		
assistant		

fuu, fu, tomu 富		
rich	house	assistant

fuku 福		
fortune	God	assistant

haba, fuku			
幅	巾	冨	
width	towel	assistant	

kizamu, koku			
刻		亥	刂
carve		seed	knife
	digging out seeds with a knife		

ka		
可	can ✂'t	can ✂'t
can	#may #can	

kawa		
河	可	氵
river	can	water
	a river in which water can flow	

ka, nan, nani 何		可
how	people / can	

people can do it. how?

ka, ni 荷		何	
load	hand	how	

ki 奇	可	
odd	can	big

eat grass. can be this big? odd..

ki, yori, yoseru 寄		奇	
close by side	house	odd big	

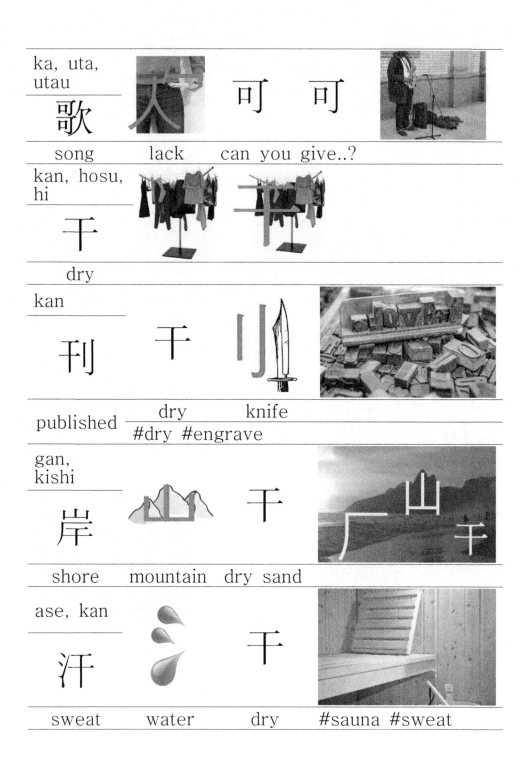

ka, uta, utau 歌	可 可	
song	lack	can you give..?

kan, hosu, hi 干		
dry		

kan 刊	干 刂	
published	dry knife	
	#dry #engrave	

gan, kishi 岸	干	
shore	mountain dry sand	

ase, kan 汗	干	
sweat	water dry	#sauna #sweat

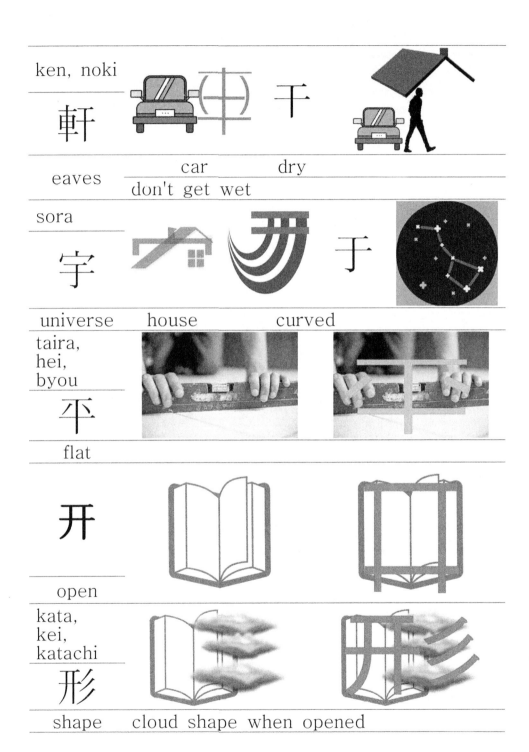

ken, noki		
軒	car	dry
eaves	don't get wet	

sora		
宇	house	curved
universe		

taira, hei, byou	
平	
flat	

开	
open	

kata, kei, katachi	
形	
shape	cloud shape when opened

ken, togu		
研		
research	the research of planets	

gata, kei				
型				
type	open	knife	soil	
	plowing type			

amai, kan			
甘		甘	甘	甘
sweet	mouth	two plus	

ushitora		
艮		
limit		

kon, ne		
根		艮
root	wood	limit

gin, shirogane 銀		艮
silver	gold　　　　limit	
	not gold, but silver	

shirizoku, tai, shirizokeru 退		艮
return	walk　　　　limit	

kagiru, gen 限		艮
limit	hill　　　　limit	

me 眼		艮
eye	eye　　　　limit	
	eyes with limited vision	

yoi, ryō 良	艮　　　良　　　良	
good	limit　　　go beyond	
	to go beyond the limits	

musume			
娘		良	
daughter	female	good	

kuu, shoku, taberu		
食	良	
food	good	cover
	to cover up the goods and make food	

in, nomu		
飲	食	
drinking	food	lack
	#lack of food #thirsty #drinking	

kitsu		
喫		
enjoy		

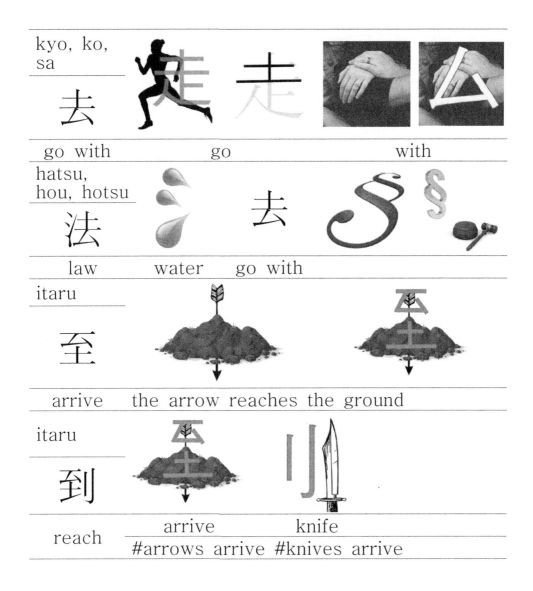

kyo, ko, sa			
去	go with	go	with

hatsu, hou, hotsu		
法	law	water go with

itaru	
至	arrive the arrow reaches the ground

itaru	
到	arrive knife
reach	#arrows arrive #knives arrive

taosu, tou		
倒		
collapse		

shitsu, muro		
室		
room	home · arrive	
	#arrive at home #get to the room	

dou			
堂			
hall	palm	earth	

oku, ya		
屋		
shop	cart	arrive

iru, kyo			
居			
	stay	cart	ancient

kyoku			
局		口	
chessboard	#measure #ruler	square plate	#situation #bureau

tei, doro			
泥			
	mud		

ichi, shi			
市	巾		
city	towel #market #city		

sē 制		
manufacture	#hand(ㅗ) #market(市) #make(knife, リ)	

sē 製	制 衣	
made	manufacture	clothing

satsu, suri 刷		中	リ
printing	#cart #bundle	#towel #paper	#knife #carve

nuno, fu 布	中	⟩
textile	#towel #textile	hand

kowa, fu			
怖	小	布	
fear	heart	textile	

ki			
希	メ	布	
rare	marked	textile	

ketsu		
夬		
open		

kimeru, ketsu, kimaru			
決			夬
decision	water		open

kai		
快		
quick	his heart is already in the car	

kyou, miyako, kei 京		
the capital		

suzushii, ryou, suzumu 涼	+ 京	
cool	water capital	

kei 景	京	
scenery	sun capital	

tsuku 就	尤 京	
employment	special city	

ketsu, musubu, yuu 結	口	
conclusion soldier word thread		

shuu, mawari 周		同	周
circumference	together		plus

shiraberu, chou, totonou 調	言	周	
tone	speak	circumference	

shuu 週		周	
week	walk	circumference	

ko, furui 古		
ancient		

ko 故	古	攴=攵
	ancient	to hit with a stick
reason	an ancient shaman hit the ground with a stick when he asked God why ⇨ reason	

karasu, ko, kare 枯	木	古	
withering	wood	ancient	

ku, kurushii, nigai 苦	艹	古	
painful	grass	ancient	

katai, ko, katameru 固	口	古	
solid	fence	ancient	

ko 個	イ	固	
individual	person	solid	

even in a hard situation...

ko, mizuumi 湖	氵	古	月	
lake	water	ancient	moon	

koku, tsugeru 告		
tell		

zou, tsukuru 造		
create		

舌	十	1,000	千	
tongue	ten	thousand		sound
	a tongue that makes a thousand sounds			

wa, hanashi, hanasu 話		舌
talk	speak	tongue

katsu 活	氵	舌	
living	water	tongue	

sen, saki	
先	
first	

arai, sen	
洗	
wash	water first
	#soap first? #water first?

kotsu, hone	
骨	
bone	bone body
	bones in the body

ayamachi, ka, sugiru	
過	
excess bone eat	

kou, ku, gu

工

engineering

巩

smash

osoreru,
kyou,
osoroshii

恐 巩

fear   smash   heart

take, chiku

竹

bamboo

kizuku,
chiku

築

construction bamboo   smash   wood

isao, kō 功	工	力		
merits	work	power		
	#work powerfully #achievement			

o, kegasu, kitanai 汚				モ
dirty	water		choke	

ayamaru, go 誤				人
#wrong	speak	#crooked #incorrect		person

betsu, wakareru, wakeru 別			刂	
different	#dissection #different types			

kyou, tomo 共	炎	共	共	
together	put one's hands together			

kyou, tomo, sonaeru 供		共	
supply	people	together	

erabu, sen 選		共	
selection	gather	together	

abaku, bou 暴			
sudden	water and light burst together suddenly		

baku 爆		暴	
explosion	fire	sudden	

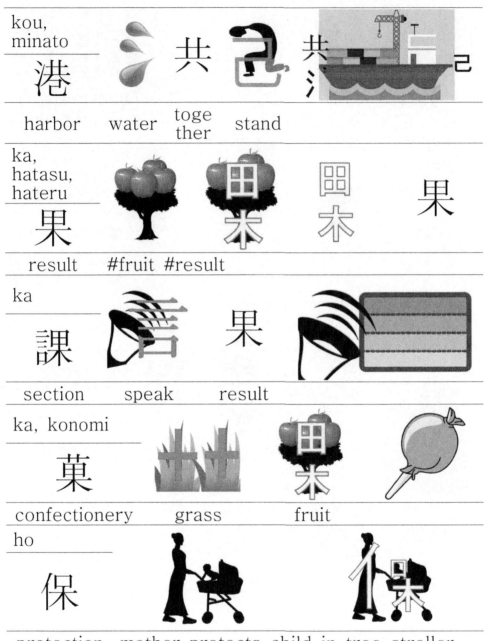

kou, minato 港			
harbor	water	together	stand

ka, hatasu, hateru 果			
result	#fruit	#result	

ka 課			
section	speak	result	

ka, konomi 菓			
confectionery	grass	fruit	

ho 保		
protection	mother protects child in tree stroller	

kan 官 official	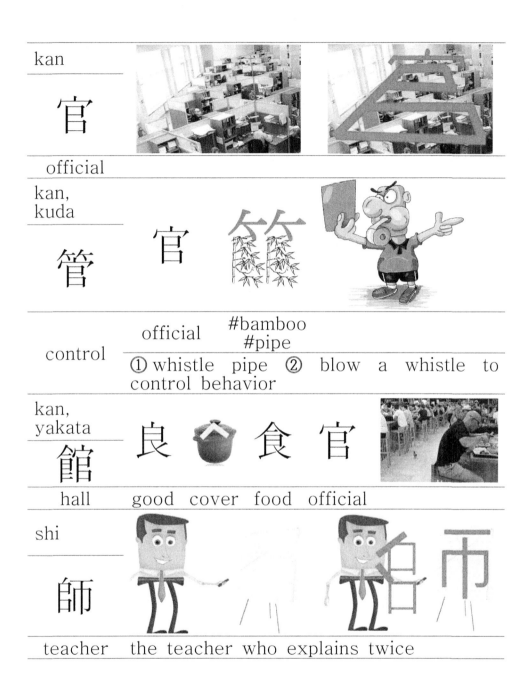	
kan, kuda 管 control	官　筍　箚 official #bamboo #pipe	
	① whistle pipe ② blow a whistle to control behavior	
kan, yakata 館 hall	良　🍲　食　官 good cover food official	
shi 師 teacher	the teacher who explains twice	

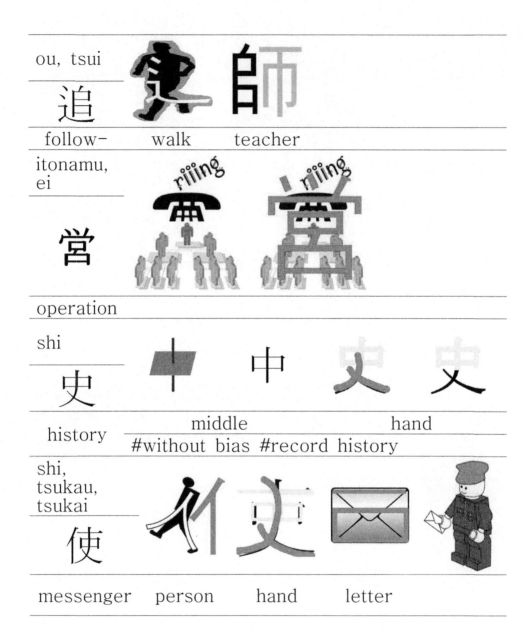

ou, tsui		
追	隶	師
follow-	walk	teacher

itonamu, ei		
営		
operation		

shi			
史	十	中	史 史
history	middle		hand
	#without bias #record history		

shi, tsukau, tsukai				
使				
messenger	person	hand	letter	

- 144 -

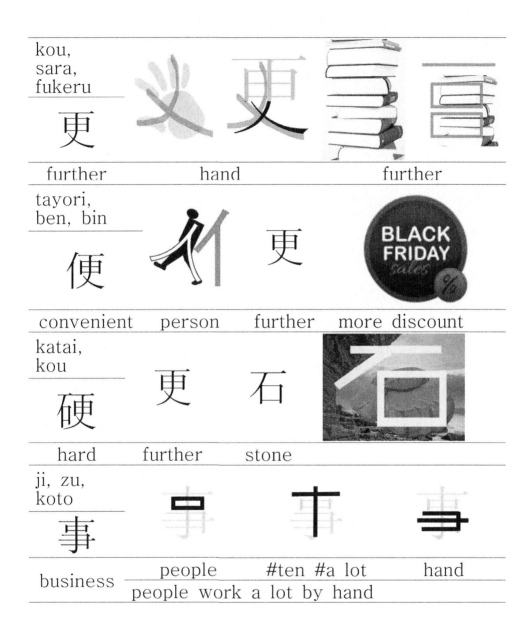

kou, sara, fukeru 更			
further	hand	further	

tayori, ben, bin 便			
convenient	person	further	more discount

katai, kou 硬			
hard	further	stone	

ji, zu, koto 事			
business	people	#ten #a lot	hand
	people work a lot by hand		

shou, meshi			
召			
convene	mouth	knife	invite

shou, maneku			
招		召	
invite	hand	convene	

shou			
紹		召	
introduce	thread	convene	

shou, teru, tereru				
照	召			灬
illuminate	convene	Sun	fire	

call the sun and fire to shine

koeru, chou, kosu 超		召	
exceed	run	convene	

ム			
together			

shi, watashi, watakushi 私	千	ム	
private	rice	together	

harau, futsu 払		ム	
payment	hand	together	

futsu, hotoke 仏		ム	
Buddha	people	together	

kou, hiroi, hiromeru 広		ム	
wide	building	together	

kou 鉱		広	
mine	gold	wide	

dai, tai 台			
table		together	mouth
	a table we can eat together		

ji, chi, naosu 治		台	
govern	oil	table	govern oil

shi, hajimeru			
始	女	台	
start	woman	table	life start

iku, sodatsu, sodateru			
育	子	𠫓	育
upbringing			

nagasu, ryū, nagareru			
流	氵	育	
stream	water	grow	flow

shin, mi			
身		身	身
body			

i			
射	身	手	射
shooting	body	hand	

- 149 -

in, hiku, hikeru		
引		
pull		

kyou, gou, tsuyoi			
強			
strength			

ori, setsu, oru			
折			
occasion	hand	#axe #mark	
	#valentine's day #birthday...		

kin, kon, chikai			
近			
near	walk	#axe #mark	
	a bear nearby		

inoru, ki			
祈			
prayer	god	axe	

sho, tokoro			
所			
place	door	#axe #mark	

shin, atarashii		
新		
new	new sprout on a cut tree	

shin, oya, shitashii			
親			
parent	taking care of a sprout	taking care of child	

hyou, hei			
兵			
soldiers	axe	hand	
	#an axe in his hand #soldiers		

shitsu			
質			
quality	money	mark	check twice

kin, gon, tsutomeru			
勤		
work		

katai, nan, muzukashii		
難		
difficult	#heavy #even birds...	

kan, han		
漢		
the Han Dynasty		

kon, kin, ima 今			
today	#combine #pile up		time
	#time is piled up #reaches today		

nen 念	今		
think	today	heart	
	#today #love #think		

gan, fukumu, fukumeru 含	今		
contain	today	mouth	keep in mouth

tsukasa, shi 司		口	
manage	order		director

kō 后	司 ⇨ 司 司 ┊ 后 后 ⇨ 后
afterwards	

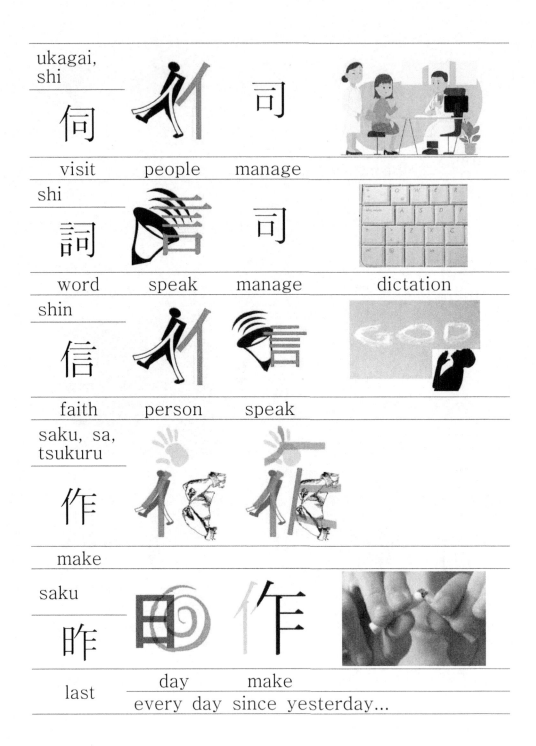

ukagai, shi			
伺	亻	司	
visit	people	manage	

shi			
詞	言	司	
word	speak	manage	dictation

shin		
信	亻	言
faith	person	speak

saku, sa, tsukuru		
作		
make		

saku		
昨	日	作
last	day	make

every day since yesterday...

atsu, kou				
厚				
thick	like pregnant			

kyuu, ku, hisashi				
久	人	人		
long time	person		wait for a long time	

oyobi			
及	人	人	及
reach	person	grab	

kyuu			
級	及		
grade	reach	#string #line	grade along line

kyuu, suu			
吸	及	口	
suck	reach	mouth	

kyou,
sakebu

叫　口

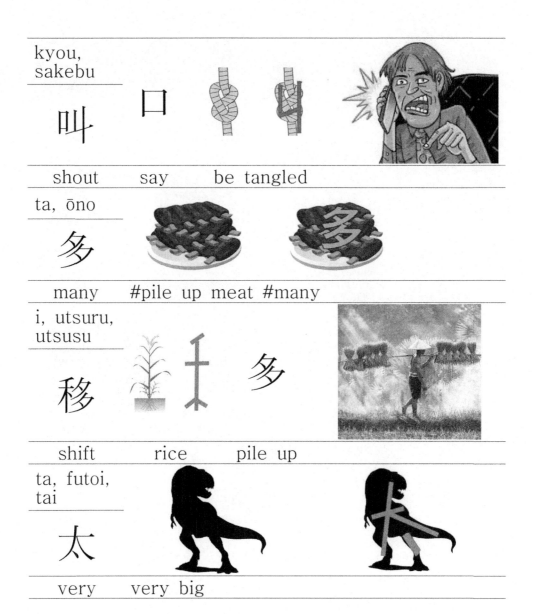

shout　say　be tangled

ta, ōno

多

many　#pile up meat #many

i, utsuru,
utsusu

移

shift　rice　pile up

ta, futoi,
tai

太

very　very big

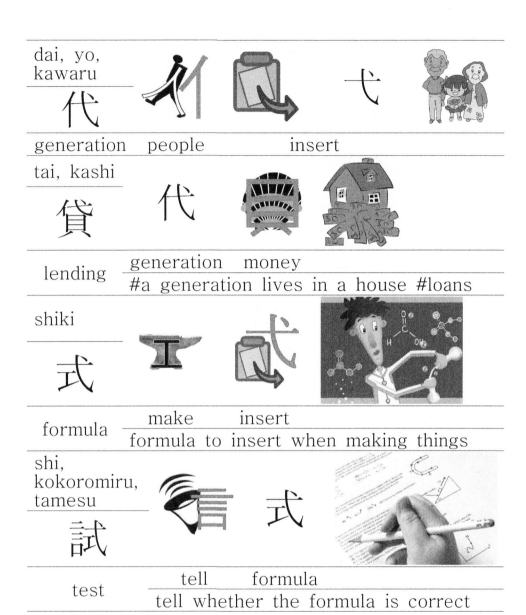

dai, yo, kawaru 代			
generation	people	insert	

tai, kashi 貸	代		
lending	generation money		
	#a generation lives in a house #loans		

shiki 式			
formula	make insert		
	formula to insert when making things		

shi, kokoromiru, tamesu 試			
test	tell formula		
	tell whether the formula is correct		

bu, mu 武	正	弋	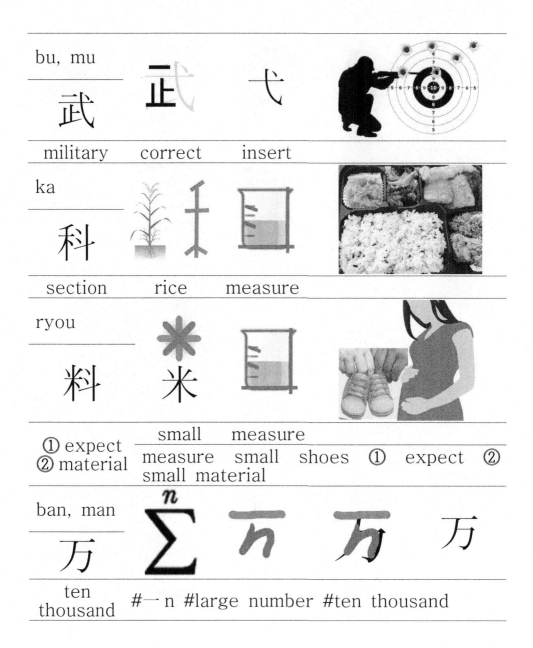
	correct	insert	
	military		
ka 科			
	section	rice	measure
ryou 料	米		
① expect ② material	small measure measure small shoes ① expect ② small material		
ban, man 万	$\sum_{n}$		
ten thousand	#一 n #large number #ten thousand		

- 158 -

hou, kata 方	square	#plow #direction
#square #direction	square	① square ② to set the direction of a plow

otozureru, hou, tazuneru 訪	ask	direction
investigate	ask opinion in many directions	

fusegu, bou 防	hill	direction
defend		

bou, botsu 坊	earth	direction
mischievous boy		

ritsu, ryuu, tatsu 立			
stand			

i, kurai 位	person	立 stand	
position	person	stand	

kyuu, naki 泣	water	立 stand	
crying	water	stand	

nami, hei, naraberu 並	立立 standing	並 ordinary	
ordinary	standing	ordinary	

fu, hiroshi			
普	並	日	
general	ordinary	Sun	general sunshine

bin, kame			
瓶	并	瓦	
bottle	side by side	tile	
	side by side like tiles		

禺	日	厶	冂	
meet	Sun	together	table	

guu, tama			
偶	亻	禺	
couple	people	meet	

guu, sumi			
隅	阝	禺	
corner	hill	meet	

hayashi, rin 林 forest		

kin 禁 forbidden	林 forest	show #only show the forest #forbidden to show..

ma, magaku 磨 milling	

reki 歴 history	 reverse forest stop stop and go back to the forest...

shin, mori 森			
woods			

sasaeru, shi 支	＋	⺌	又
support	plus		hand
	support by adding hands		

eda, shi 枝		木	支
branch	tree		support
	branches that support the tree		

gi, waza 技	拝	支	
skill	hand	support	

ken, miru, mi 見	見 (eye over legs)	見
see		

arawasu, gen 現	(beads) 見	(camera)
reveal	#bead #lens	see

kan 観	(bird) 見	(bird) 隹 見
view	#don't touch	#just view

ai, sou, shou 相	木 相 (eye)	(tree and camera)
photo	tree	eye

so, sou 想	相		心
	photo		heart
miss you	I miss you in my heart when I see the photo		

hako 箱		箱	竹	相
		bamboo		photo
box	a bamboo box in which to put a picture			

ken 県				
prefecture	eye	tree		

mon, kado 門	
gate	

- 165 -

kai, hiraku, akeru 開	門		开
open	gate	open	

hatsu, abaku, tatsu 発		癶		
departure	walk	open		

mon, tou 問	門		
question	gate	speak	

bun, kiku 聞	門		
hear	gate	ear	

shimeru, tojiru, hei	門	才	
閉			
closed	gate	cut wood	

kan, aida, ma	門	田	
間			
between	gate	Sun	

kan	間	筍	
簡			
simple	between	bamboo	
	#between lines #brief guide.		

关			关	关
shut				

kan, seki	門	关	
関			
barrier	gate	shut	

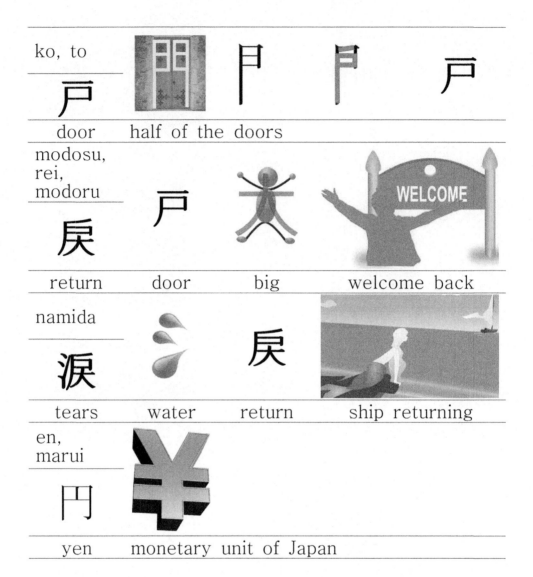

ko, to			
戸			
door	half of the doors		

modosu, rei, modoru			
戻			
return	door	big	welcome back

namida			
涙			
tears	water	return	ship returning

en, marui			
円			
yen	monetary unit of Japan		

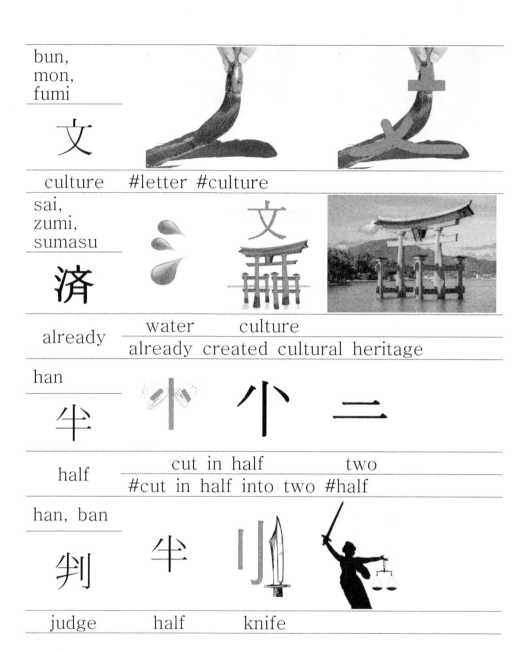

bun, mon, fumi 文		
culture	#letter #culture	
sai, zumi, sumasu 済	water	culture
already	already created cultural heritage	
han 半	cut in half	two
half	#cut in half into two #half	
han, ban 判		
judge	half	knife

sorasu, han, tan 反			
	anti-	reverse	hand
kaesu, pen, kaeru 返		反	
	return	walk	anti-
shoku 食	SPEED LIMIT	良	
	food	limit	#beyond the limits #good	cover
han, meshi 飯	食	反	
	food	food	anti-	increase immunity
saka, han 坂	土	反	
	slope	earth	anti-	

ita, han, ban 板	木	反	
board	wood	anti-	not fresh

han 版	朾	反	
printing plate	a piece of wood	anti-	#anti-surface #engrave
a print plate made of a piece of wood			

han 販		反	
sales	money	anti-	price goes down

fu, bu 不			不
do not	we must not go out anymore		

sakazuki, hai 杯	木	不	
cup	wood	not	not wood
ina, hi 否	不	口	
no	do not	say	
yaku 約		#wrap	#make a
appointment	#connect promise		#make a dot
teki, mato 的	白	ク	、 ⊕
target	white	wrap	dot

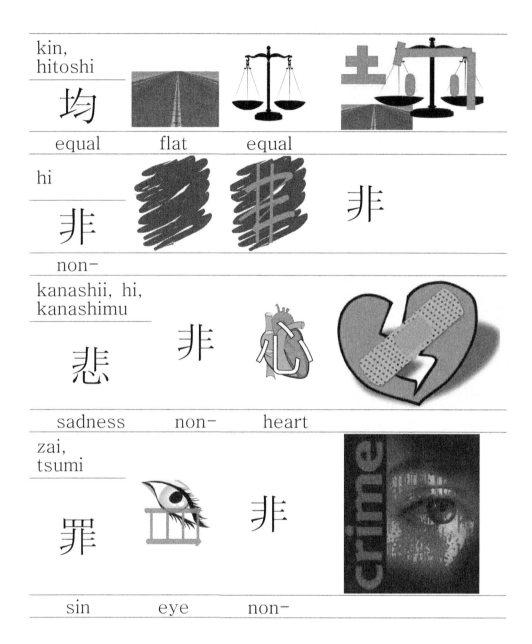

kin, hitoshi 均		
equal	flat	equal

hi 非		
non-		

kanashii, hi, kanashimu 悲		
sadness	non-	heart

zai, tsumi 罪		
sin	eye	non-

ヒ			レ
spoon, knife			

katamuku,
kei,
katamukeru

傾

| | tilt | people | knife | page |

abura,
shi

脂

| | fat | body | knife |

sasu,
shi, yubi

指

| | indicate | #eye exam | #hand | #indicate |

ka, ke, bakeru 化	人	人ㄚ	仆	化

transform #change into #convert

ka, ge, hana 花	仆	化	(grass image)	++

flower	transform		grass	

flowers blooming in the grass

ka 貨	化	(coin image)	(money image)

currency	transform	money	

kuraberu, hi 比	(glass with spoon image)	ヒ	ヒヒ ⇒ 比

compare	compare two spoons		

hi 批	比	扌	扌

criticism	compare	#hand #indicate	

indicate a mistake by comparison

kai, mina			
皆	比	白	
all	compare	white	#white #comparison #all

kai			
階	ß	皆	
floor	hill	all	

kon, majiru, mazaru		
混	比	
mix	abreast	

nou			
能			能
ability			

tai		
態	能	心
attitude	ability	heart

shun, haru				
春				
spring	spring when sprouts grow			

ka, natsu				
夏				
summer	hat	eye	walk	

ai				
愛				
love	hand	cover	heart	walk
	#in chest #with hands..			

sugureru, you, yasashii				
優				
superiority	people	hundred	love	
	loved by hundreds of people			

shuu, aki			
秋	rice	fire	
autumn	#harvest rice #cook rice #autumn		

tou, fuyu			
冬			
winter	walk	ice	

shuu, owari, tsui		
終	#string #connect	winter
the end	winter is the end of connected seasons	

kan, samui		
寒		
cold	broken	ice floor

aratameru, aratamaru, kai				
改		己		夂
alter	stand up		#hit #fix	
	#to fix and stand up #alter			

mai, bai			
枚		夂	
sheet	wood	fix	

san, chiru, chirakasu				
散			夂	
scatter	pile up	body	hit	woofer body

shaku, seki, mukashi			
昔			
long ago	pile up	day	

shaku, kari			
借	亻	昔	
borrowing	people	long ago	for a long time, people...

seki			
籍	竹	耒	昔
registration	bamboo	register	long ago

emu, warai, shou				
笑			笑	笑
laugh	are bamboo eyebrows real? (laughs)			

夨			关	夨
shut				

sou, okuru			
送	奐	辶	夨
send	walk		close
	send and close		

- 180 -

saki				
咲		关		
bloom	speak	shut		

shu, zu, te					
手	手	拝	拝	木	又
hand					

ogamu, hai		
拝	拝手	
worship	hand + hand	

sagase, sou		
搜	拝申又	
search		

yuu, u, aru 有				
have	body		hand	
	#body #hand #have			

sai 才	木	才		
talent	cut wood to make things			

son, zon, ari 存	木 ⇨ 才 ⇨ 亻			
exist		talent		child
	#children have talent #talent exists			

ari, zai 在	亻			
exist	talent	ground		

shu, mamoru, mori 守				
guard	house	hand		

son, mura			
村	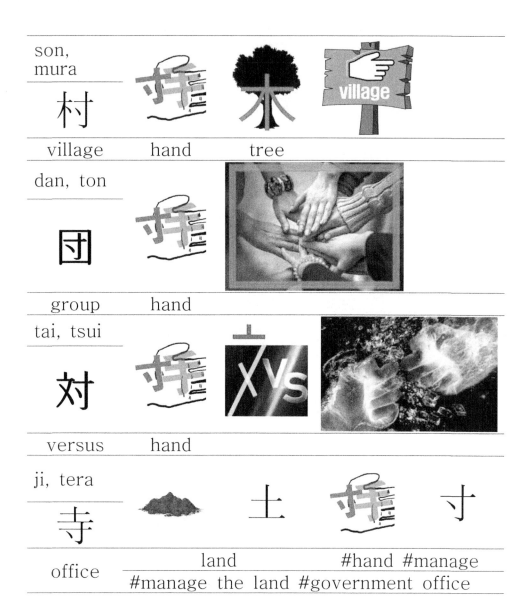		
village	hand	tree	

dan, ton		
団		
group	hand	

tai, tsui		
対		
versus	hand	

ji, tera			
寺			
office	land	#hand #manage	

#manage the land #government office

tai, machi			
待	彳	寺	
wait	walk	office	

tou, hitoshii			
等	寺	竹	
etc.	office	bamboo	

ji, toki			
時	日	寺	
time	day	office	

ji, mochi, moteru			
持	寺	扌	
possession	office	hand	

tsuku, fu, tsukeru 付	 
entrust	#give #hand over #entrust

fu 府	
government	building give building to give documents

fu 符	
sign	bamboo give

sou, futa 双	
double	hand hand #hands and hands #twice #double

shuu, osamaru 収			
collection	be tangled	hand	

ukaru, ju, ukeru 受			
receive	hand	hand	

nari 也	匕	丨	丁
and also	hand	and	hand
hands, hands, hands also			

ta, hoka 他	仆		也
he	people	and also	
#and also people #another #he			

chi, ji			
地	也	土	
land	and also	soil	soil, also soil
ike, chi			
池	⟩	也	
pond	water	and also	water, also water
son, toutobu, tattobu			
尊	酉	廾	
honor	vessel	hand	
fu			
婦	女	帚	
woman	female	broom	

sou, haku 掃		
sweep	hand	broom

ki, kaeru 帰		
return		

shutsu, dasu, de 出			
out	log out #come out #go out		

kutsu, horu 掘			
digging	hand	cart	out

setsu, tsugu 接		 立 扌女
connect	#woman(女) #stand(立) #hand(扌)	

sai, zuma 妻			 扌 女
	wife	hand	female

koori, hyou, hi 氷		水	氷
	ice	water	ice

ei, nagai 永				永
forever	the sun is forever			

ei, oyogu 泳	water	forever	
swim	always in the water...		
izumi, sen 泉	white	water	
fountain			
sen 線		泉	
line	thread	fountain	
	#thread #up like a fountain		
gen, hara 原	reverse	white	small
original	#reverse #white and small..		
minamotono 源	原		
source	origin	water	
	a origin of water		

gan, negai			*Wish list*
願	原	頁	
wish	original	page	original mind..

tate			
盾			
shield			

jika, choku, naosu			
直	盾	自	直
straight	#set a shield upright #straight		

ueru, uwaru, shoku		
植	木	直
plants	tree	straight
	plant a tree straight	

atai, chi, ne		
値	イ	直
value	people	straight

oke, chi			
置		直	
position	eye	straight	

shin, ma, makoto				
真	十		目	六
	ten	eye		table
true	#check ten times with eyes on the table #real #true			

shin, jin				
臣		用	臣	臣
servant	servant who only looks down			

katai, ken				
堅	臣		土	
firm	servant	hand	soil	

kashikoi, ken				
賢	臣			
wise	servant	hand	money	growing money

kan', mi 看				
watch	hand	eye		

tami, min 民			
	eye	can't open one's eyes	
people	#can't open one's eyes #people who have not learned ancient times		

nemui, min, nemuru 眠					
sleep	eye	people			

hin, shina

品

commodity

sou

燥 品

dry | fire | wood | comm odity | hot-air product

misao

操

manipulation

nai, bou, mou

亡

broken

bou, wasureru

忘 亡

forget | broken | heart

isogashii, bou

忙 亡

busy | heart | broken

nozomu, bou, mochi 望 hope	I hope the broken bead recovers at night	
ara, kou, areru 荒 rough	grass broken flow rough water that sweeps the grass	
gen, koto, iu 言 speak		
go, kataru, katari 語 word	speak five mouth 5-year-old reading	

kisou, kyou, seri 競			
competition	stand	breathe	run

bai 倍		
twice	twice the size of the mouth	

bu 部				
	hill	stand	word	
section	#a word standing on hill #milestones # section			

akinau, shou 商				口
	a product		say	
business	say something to sell a product			

商			冂	
	pot	stand	long time	fence

shizuku, teki, shitataru				
滴			商	
drop		water		pot

teki				
適			商	
suitable	walk		pot	

#walk #suitable nutrition

kun		
訓		
lesson		

kei, hakaru			
計		+	
total	speak	plus	

san 算	算	筭	筭	算
calculate				

you, mochiiru 用				
use	use a bucket			

sonaeru, bi, sonawaru				
備				
	亻	用	丷	
prepare	people	use	hand	reverse

isamu, yuu 勇				
		力		
courage	a bucket with a handle	power		

itai, tsuu, itamu			
痛			
pain	bucket	sick	

tsuu, tooru, toori			
通			
through	bucket	walk	

odori, you, odoru			
踊			
dance	legs	bucket	

hajime			
甫	用		
assist	use	hand	

oginau, ho			
補		甫	
supplement	clothes	assist	mend

tsukamaru, ho, toru 捕			
capture	hand	assist	

sha, kuruma 車	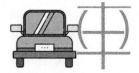		
car			

nan, yawaraka, yawarakai 軟			
soft	car	lack	
	#hard car	#lack of softness	

ku, ko 庫			
warehouse	building	car	

gun			
軍	車	冖	
military	vehicle	cover	

tsuraneru, ren, tsureru			
連	車		
connect	#vehicle #wheel	walk	

un, hakobu			
運		軍	
luck	walk	military	

karui, kei, karoyaka			
軽	車		土
light weight	car	hand	earth

経		
kyou, heru, kei		

economy

thread	hand	earth

#thread a needle #manage #economically

径		
kē		

diameter   #build a road #path #diameter

専		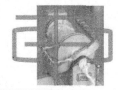	
sen, mobbara			

exclusive   only one direction   hand

薄			専	
usu, haku				

thin

grass	water	only

only ate water and grass...

谷		
koku, tani		

valley

hoshii, yoku, hossuru 欲		
greed	overflow	lack
	#overflowing! #still lack?	

abiru, yoku 浴	谷	
bath	water overflow	

you 容	谷	
appearance	house overflow	
	house full of looks	

toku, you, tokeru 溶	容	
melt	water appearance	

u, ha, hane		
羽		
feather		

shuu, ju, narai	羽	
習		
practice	feather white	
	white uniform. as light as a feather.	

yoku	羽	
翌		
next day	feather stand	
	effective from the next day	

you	日 羽	
曜		
day of the week	day feather bird like feather	

- 204 -

taku 濯				
rinse	water	feather	bird	

jaku, yowai 弱			
weak	feather falling from the bow ⇨ weak		

gaku, raku, tanoshii 楽				
ease	white	line	wood	
	#music #enjoyable #ease			

kusuri, yaku 薬		楽	
medicine	grass	ease	ease pain

in 員 member	money	group	membership
sokonau, son, sokoneru 損 loss	員 member	hand	weight loss
men, wata 綿 cotton	thread	white	fiber
e, kai, mawaru 回 return			

tomeru, ryuu, ru			
留			
stay	field	tool	
	#farm #tool #cultivate #stay		

bou			
貿			
trade	tool	money	

hiki, hitsu			
匹			
animal counter	four	4 or more	

kanarazu, hitsu			
必			
must	heart	pledge	
	#pledge with one's heart #must		

mitsu				
密				
dense	house	must	mountain	building forest

richi, ritsu			
律			
law	walk	pen	suspect

sho, kaku			
書			
book	pen	speak	written story

hitsu, fude		
筆		
brush	bamboo	pen

ken, kon, tate		
建		
build	pen	design

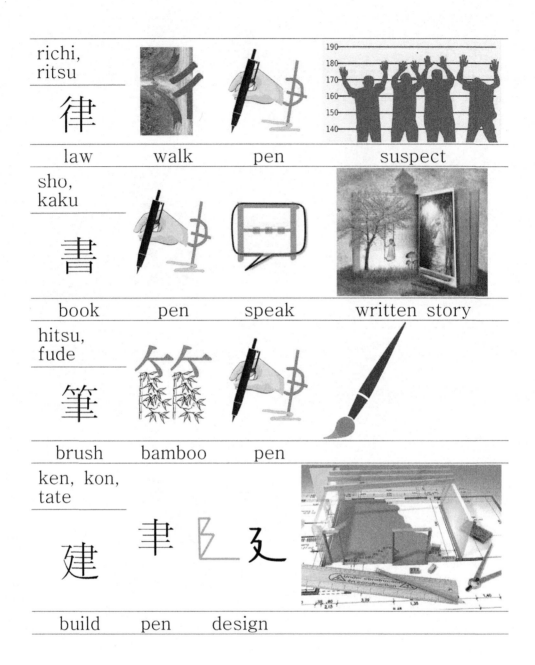

ataeru, yo 与				
and	#one	and	one	#and

sha, utsushi 写			
copy	cover	and	#open cover and copy #photo

ga, kaku 画		
picture	paint	flowerpot

i, koromo 衣			
clothing	clothes tied with string		

i, e			
依	イ	衤	衣
depend	people	clothes	

dai			
代	イ		弋
generation	people	insert	

tai, fukuro			
袋	代	衣	
bag	generation	clothes	suitcase

ura, ri			
裏	衣		里
back	clothes	village	

arawasu, hyou, omote			
表	衣	土	
surface	clothes	soil	#surface #expression

sō 壮	木	宇	
magnificent	wood	weapon	soldier

shou, sou, yosoou 装	壮	衣	
dress	magnificent	clothes	dress magnificent clothes

en' 袁	ネ	ネ	圭	㞡	袁
stretch					

en, sono 園	袁	口	
garden	stretch	encircle	

en, on, tooi 遠	実	袁	
far away	walk	stretch	

歹		匕	歹

bad   #broken bones #dead #bad

匕		レ

#spoon #knife

shi,
shinu

死	歹	匕	

dead   bones   knife

retsu

列	歹	刂	

sort   bones   section

tatoeru, rei			
例	亻	列	
example	person	sort	

kou, muku, mukou			
向	冂	口	
toward	fence	people	

jou, tsune, toko			
常		巾	
often	palm	towel	#hands #towels #often

shou			
賞			
prize	palm	money	

tou			
党		儿	
clique	palm	people	palm-sized clique

ataru, tou, ateru 当	finger	hand	
#should #when	we **should** fix the roof **when** it's not raining		

gaku, manabu 学			
learn	learn for glory		

oboeru, kaku 覚		見	学 / 龸
awakening	see	learn	
	#see #learn #awakening		

arasou, sou, arasoi 争			争
fight	#spear #hand #fight		

sotsu 卒	 		
graduation			

kau, kou, majiru 交		✕	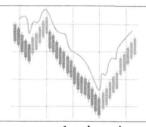
alternate	six	cross	repeated six times

kou 校		交	
school	wood	alternate	#alternate #wooden chairs

kou 郊	交		
countryside	alternate		hill

kiku, kou			
効	交	力	
effective	alternate	power	power of alternate

kyuu, motomeru			
求		寸	ハ
begging	hand		hand
	#beseech	#request	#beg

kyuu, tama			
球		求	
ball	bead	#beg #hand	

kyuu, sukui			
救		求 夊	
salvation	bead	hit	

kyou, oshieru 教		
teach		

kazu, suu, kazoeru 数		
number	woman 女　hit 夊	number 米

ji, mimi 耳	
ear	

chi, haji, hazukashii 恥	耳		
shame	ear	heart	cover ears...

shu, tori 取		
take	#receive #take #obtain	

sai, mottomo 最		
most	speak take #cheer #take #most high	

ji, shi, mizukara 自		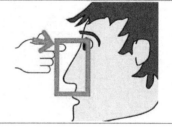
self		

hana, bi 鼻	   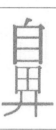
nose	nose

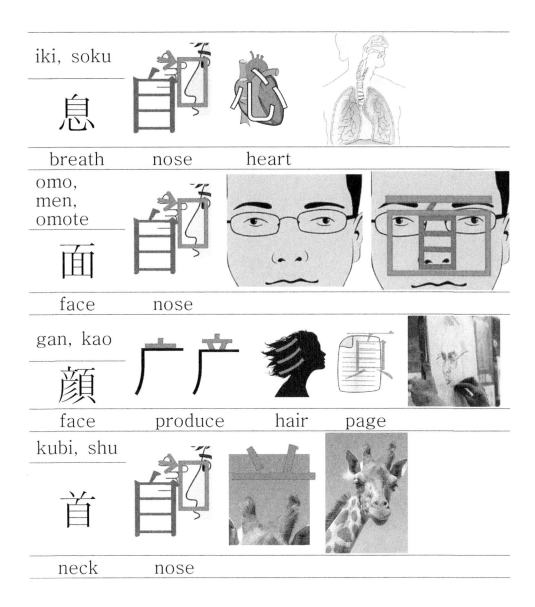

iki, soku				
息				
breath	nose	heart		
omo, men, omote				
面				
face	nose			
gan, kao				
顔				
face	produce	hair	page	
kubi, shu				
首				
neck	nose			

dou, tou, michi			
道		首	
road	walk	neck	long as neck...

tou, michibiku			
導	道		
guidance	road	hand	

atari, hen, be			
辺			
edge	walk	knife	

zen, mae			
前			
forward			

yu

輸

transport　　car

do, taku, tabi

度

degree

to, watari, watasu

渡

cross river　　water　　degree

seki

席

seat

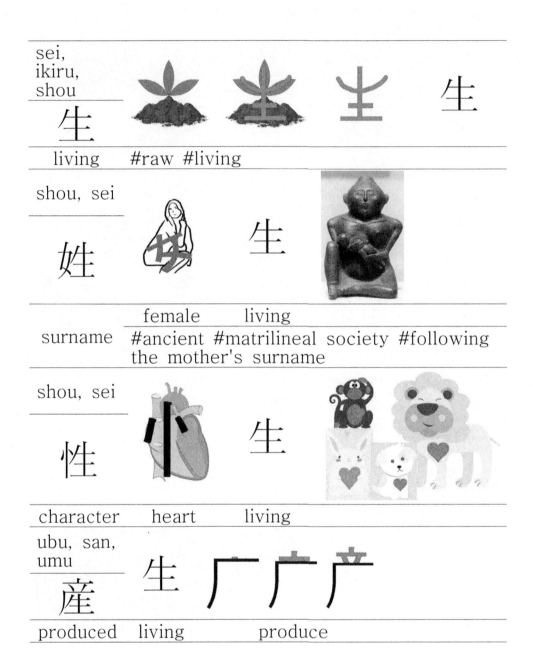

sei,
ikiru,
shou

生

living   #raw #living

shou, sei

姓

      female   living

surname   #ancient #matrilineal society #following the mother's surname

shou, sei

性

character   heart   living

ubu, san,
umu

産

produced   living   produce

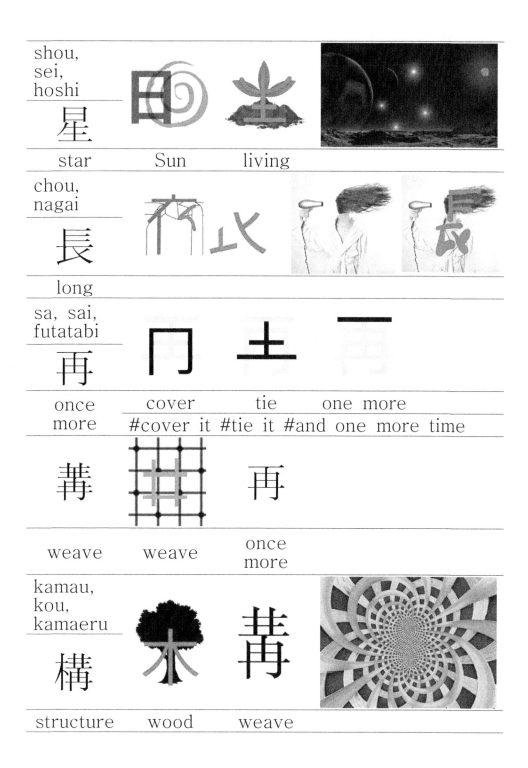

shou, sei, hoshi 星		
star	Sun	living

chou, nagai 長		
long		

sa, sai, futatabi 再		
once more	cover	tie	one more
	#cover it	#tie it	#and one more time

講		
weave	weave	once more

kamau, kou, kamaeru 構		
structure	wood	weave

kou			
講	言	冓	
lecture	speak	weave	

sai			
才	木	才	
talent	#cut wood #make things #talent #genius		

zai			
材	木	才	
material	wood	cut wood	

sai, zai			
財	貝	才	
goods	money talent #calling guest #selling goods		

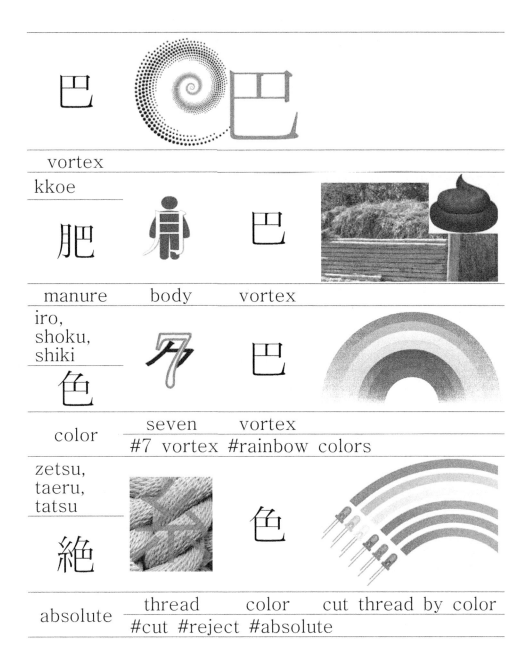

巴		
vortex		

肥	身	巴
manure	body	vortex

色	7	巴
color	seven	vortex

#7 vortex #rainbow colors

絶	糸	色
absolute	thread	color

cut thread by color

#cut #reject #absolute

kkoe

iro,
shoku,
shiki

zetsu,
taeru,
tatsu

setsu, sai, kire 切			七
cut	knife	to cut	

hatsu, sho, hajime 初			
beginning	#clothes #shell	#knife #cut	cut shell...

kei 系			
system	touch	thread	

kakari, kei, kakaru 係		系	
person in charge	people	system	

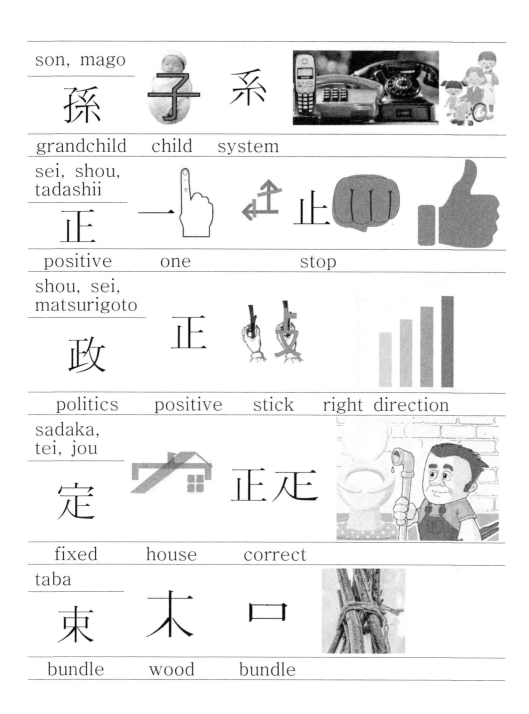

son, mago		
孫	子	系
grandchild	child	system

sei, shou, tadashii		
正	一	止
positive	one	stop

shou, sei, matsurigoto			
政	正	攴	
politics	positive	stick	right direction

sadaka, tei, jou		
定		正疋
fixed	house	correct

taba		
束	木	口
bundle	wood	bundle

sei			
整	束	正	攴
arrange	bundle	correct	hit

hisage			
提	扌	日	正疋
proposal	hand	sun	positive

dai			
題	是	頁	
title	proposal	page	

sa			
査	木		
inspection	wood	add	

jo, tasukeru, tasukaru			
助	力		
help	strength	add	

so 祖			
ancestor	show	add	

kumi, so, kumu 組			
group	thread	add	

jou, tatami, tatamu 畳			
tatami	field cover add		Japanese straw floor covering

sou, hashiru 走	
run	

etsu, koeru, koshi		
越		
jump over		

kuro				
黒				
black	charcoal	earth	fire	scorched

hi		
曾		
steam		

zou, nikui, nikumu		
憎		曾 
hatred	heart	stcam

okuru, zou, sou		
贈		曾 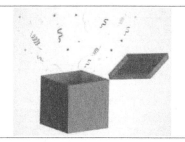
gift	money	steam

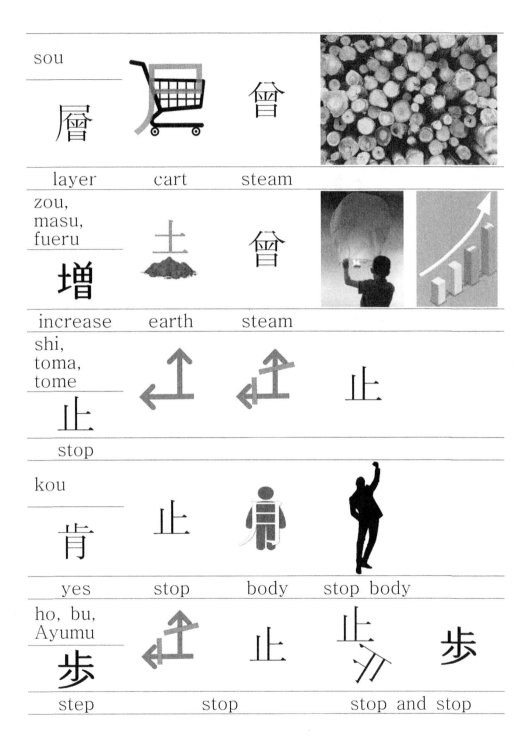

sou 層	cart	steam	
layer	cart	steam	
zou, masu, fueru 増	earth	steam	
increase	earth	steam	
shi, toma, tome 止			止
stop			
kou 肯	止 stop	body	stop body
yes	stop	body	stop body
ho, bu, Ayumu 歩	止	止	歩
step	stop		stop and stop

sai, sei, toshi			

歳			
age	step	director	spear

kou, furu, oriru			
降	hill	walk	foot

descend	hill	walk	foot	

to				
徒				
people	walk	earth	stop	gathering

kizashi, ichou, kizasu		
兆		

symptoms

tou, nigeru, nogasu			
逃		兆	
escape	walk	symptoms	

ashi, soku, tariru	
足	
legs	

saku, satsu	
冊	
book	

rin, wa				
輪			冊	
circle	#car #wheel	combine	book	

kokorozashi			
志	士		
purpose	soldier	heart	

shi			
仕	イ	止	
end	people	soldier	finish

koe, sei, kowa			
声	止	◎巴	
voice	soldier	vortex	

uranai, sen, shimeru		
占		
occupy		

ten, mise			
店		占	
shop	building	occupy	

ten			
点	占		
point	occupy	fire	

riku			
陸			
land	hill	earth	

ikioi, sei, zē				
勢				
force	land	bend	power	

atsui, netsu				
熱				
heat	land	bend	fire	

juku, tsukuzuku		
熟		
ripe		

shou, yaki, yakeru		
焼		
grilled	fire	

kai			
貝			
money	shellfish	shiny shellfish	#money #wealth

bai, kai			
買		貝	
buy	eye	money	

hai, yabureru			
敗	貝		
defeat	money	hit	

soku			
則	貝		
rule	wealth	knife	

gawa, soku 側	イ	則	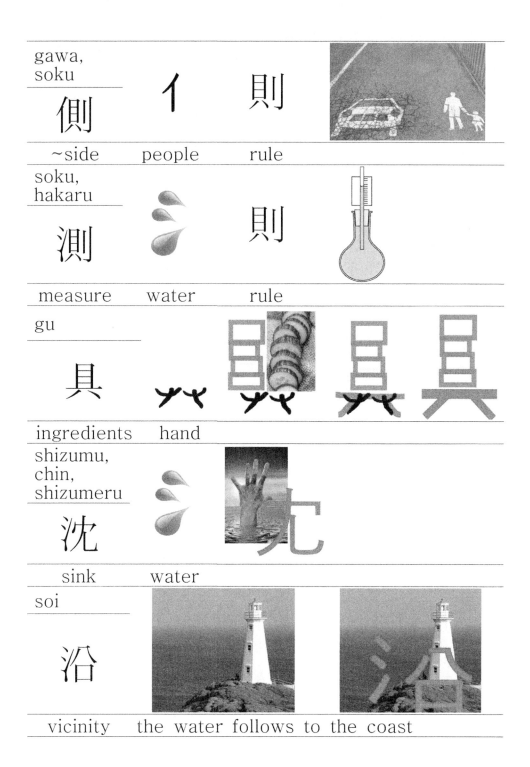
~side	people	rule	
soku, hakaru 測	氵	則	
measure	water	rule	
gu 具	ㅛ		
ingredients	hand		
shizumu, chin, shizumeru 沈	氵		
sink	water		
soi 沿			
vicinity	the water follows to the coast		

shin, fukai, fukameru 深		
deep	water	

sagasu, tan, saguru 探		
search	hand	deep

au, gou, ka 合		
combine	combine a bowl with a lid	

kyuu 給	合	
supply	combine	thread

tou,
kotaeru,
kotae

答   筝   合

| answer | bamboo | combine |

tou

塔   土   艹   合

| tower | earth | grass | combine |

rei

令   彐   卩   亼

| order | | kneel | combine |

ryou

領   令   頁

| territory | order | page |

rei			
零	雨	令	
zero	rain falls	order	
countdown in order like rain ⇨ zero			

samasu, rei, tsumetai			
冷		冫	令
cold	ice		zero
below zero temperature			

rei			
齢	歯	令	
age	tooth	order	
on the order of time...			

inochi, mei, myou			
命	口	令	
life	mouth	order	

gyou, kou, iku		
行		
walk	to walk along the intersection	

術		
technique		

jutsu

術	行 术	
art	walk technique	

jutsu, noberu

述	実 术	
description	walk technique narrate	
	broadcast technology	

sen, chi			
千	十	'	**1,000**
thousand	ten		

e, chou, omoi					
重	千	品	土		
heavy	1000	barbell	earth	barbell 1000lb	

ugoku, dou			
動	重	力	
movement	heavy	power	

tou, hatarake			
働	イ	動	
work	people	movement	

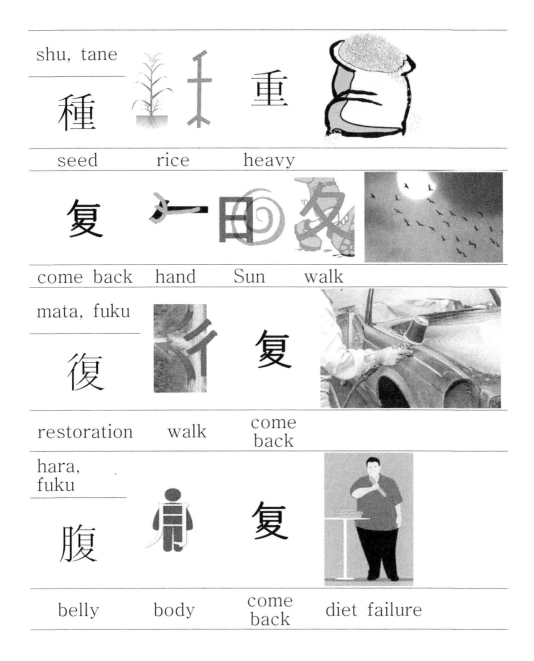

shu, tane		
種	千	重
seed	rice	heavy

复	一	日	叉
come back	hand	Sun	walk

mata, fuku		
復	彳	复
restoration	walk	come back

hara, fuku		
腹		复
belly	body	come back	diet failure

fuku 複	衣	复	
multiple	clothes	come back	layered nest

kei, kyou, ani 兄	兄		an elder brother who teaches by words
elder brother			

iwau, shuku, shuu 祝	示	兄	
celebration	show	brother	happy birthday

kyou 況	冫	兄	
situation	water	brother	what situation?
	the brothers hope it will rain		

zei, setsu, toku 説	言	兄	兑
say	say		feeling
	to say as you feel		

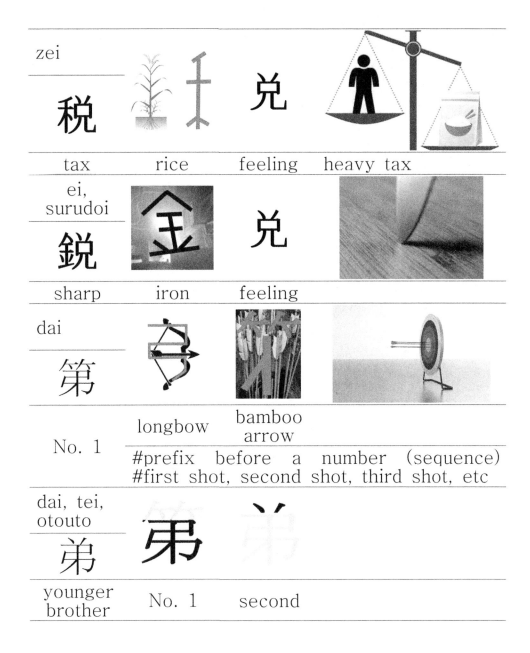

税	rice	feeling	heavy tax
zei — tax			

鋭	iron	feeling	
ei, surudoi — sharp			

第

No. 1

longbow | bamboo arrow

#prefix before a number (sequence)
#first shot, second shot, third shot, etc

弟

dai, tei, otouto — younger brother

No. 1 | second

- 245 -

kou, hikari, hikari			
光			
light			

dan			
談			
talk	speak	fire	
	sit in a campfire and talk		

kai, hai		
灰		
ash		

sumi, tan			
炭			
charcoal	mountain	ash	

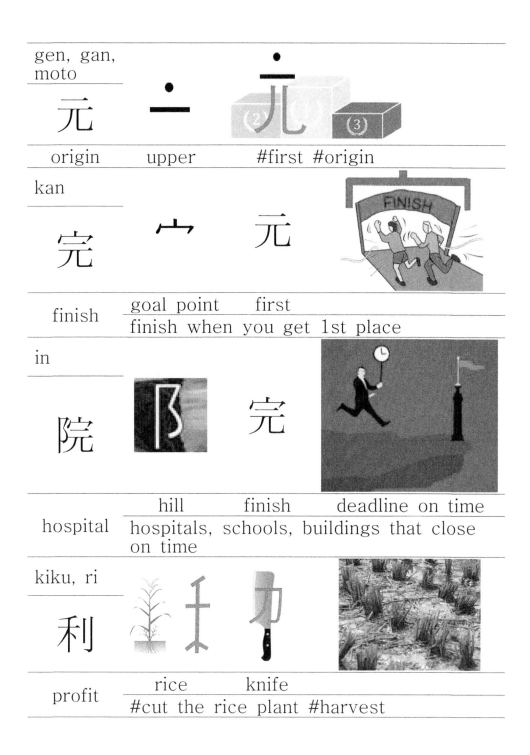

gen, gan, moto 元	· ―	·元
origin	upper	#first #origin

kan 完	宀	元
finish	goal point first
	finish when you get 1st place

in 院	阝	完
hospital	hill finish deadline on time
	hospitals, schools, buildings that close on time

kiku, ri 利	(rice plant) ⺾ (knife) 刀	
profit	rice knife
	#cut the rice plant #harvest

wa, yawaraku, nagomu 和		禾		口
		rice		mouth
and	#rice-eating mouth #be harmonious #and			

juu, nyuu, yawarakai 柔		矛		
	soft	spear	wood	

ka, kou, kaori 香		禾	日	
	scent	rice	Sun	

ki 季	子	禾	
season	child	rice	
	the season of growing young rice		

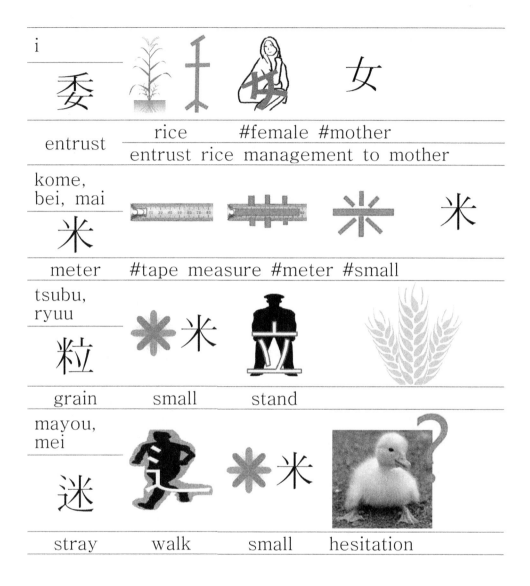

i		rice	#female #mother	女
委				
entrust		entrust rice management to mother		

kome, bei, mai				米
米				
meter	#tape measure #meter #small			

tsubu, ryuu				
粒				
grain	small	stand		

mayou, mei				
迷				
stray	walk	small	hesitation	

kotowaru, dan, tatsu 断	米		斤
cut off	small		axe
	to cut off a small thing with an axe		

shi, ha 歯	
tooth	

ban 番		
seed	small seeds flying over the field	

rai, kuru 来			
coming	insert	wood	
	spring is coming		

tobasu,
hi, tobu

飛

flight

sai

采

collect   collect from trees

sai, toru

採

picking   hand   collect

sai, na

菜

vegetable   collect   grass

otoko	男	20	ri	理	52	sa	差	43
owari	終	178	ri	立	160	sa	去	129
oya	親	151	ri	利	247	sa	査	228
oyobi	及	155	riku	陸	235	sagase	捜	181
pēji	頁	36	rin'	林	162	sai	際	72
pēji	頁	56	rin'	輪	233	sai	細	89
pen'	返	170	ritsu	率	109	sai	才	182
ppanashi	放	49	ritsu	律	208	sai	最	218
rai	頼	70	ro	路	69	sai	再	223
rai	頼	84	rō	労	20	sai	才	224
rai	来	250	rō	老	106	sai	采	251
raku	絡	68	roku	六	2	sai	採	251
ran'	乱	94	roku	録	90	sai	菜	251
ran'	卵	113	rui	類	36	saiwai	幸	82
rē	礼	94	ryaku	略	68	saka	坂	170
rē	戻	168	ryō	漁	5	sakae	栄	14
rē	例	213	ryō	両	23	sakai	境	74
rē	令	239	ryō	量	51	sakai	宇	125
rē	零	240	ryō	寮	95	sake	酒	85
rē	冷	240	ryō	了	96	sakebi	叫	156
rē	齢	240	ryō	良	127	saki	咲	181
reki	歴	162	ryō	涼	134	saku	策	85
ren	練	84	ryō	料	158	saku	作	154
ren'	連	201	ryō	領	239	saku	昨	154
retsu	列	212	ryoku	力	19	sama	様	42
ri	里	51	ryū	流	149	san'	三	1
			sa	砂	8			

Printed in Great Britain
by Amazon

17689325R00154